The 24-Hour Comedy TV Show with ChatGPT

Andrew Parry

Published by Andrew Parry, 2025.

THE 24-HOUR COMEDY TV SHOW WITH CHATGPT

First edition. May 10, 2025.

ISBN: 979-8231851485

Written by Andrew Parry.

Table of Contents

So You Want to Make People Laugh on TV

Let's be honest—if you're reading this, you've probably already made someone laugh. Maybe you've cracked up your friends during a group chat or written a tweet that got a few dozen likes. Maybe you've spent years dreaming of writing your own sitcom, the next *Brooklyn Nine-Nine*, *Ted Lasso*, or something so bizarre and brilliant it doesn't even exist yet. Or maybe you just have a really funny family and think, "This stuff writes itself." Well, it doesn't write itself. But with ChatGPT in your corner, it just might feel like it does.

Writing a television comedy series is both exhilarating and intimidating. It's not just about stringing jokes together. A successful comedy balances character development, story arcs, themes, structure, and timing with humor that lands consistently—whether it's light chuckles or full-on belly laughs. And doing all that while imagining how it will look and feel on-screen adds another layer. But that's where this book comes in. In the next 59 chapters, we're going to walk you through the process of crafting your own comedy series in a single day, with the help of a tool that never gets tired, never complains, and never eats the last cookie in the writer's room: ChatGPT.

You don't need to have written for TV before. You don't need to have a film school degree or even know how to format a script—though we'll touch on that. What you do need is a sense of humor and the willingness to dig into your weirdest, wildest, most ridiculous ideas. Comedy is a playground, and you're about to become its most ambitious new architect.

But before we dive into generating characters or plotting out episodes, we need to address something deeper: **why** you want to make people laugh in the first place. Because your "why" will shape everything about your show—from the tone, to the themes, to the kinds of stories you'll tell. Are you drawn to comedy because you want to expose something absurd about modern life? Because you want to offer comfort in hard times? Or maybe because it's the only way you know how to process your own chaos? All of that matters.

When you look at the greatest TV comedies, from *The Office* to *Fleabag*, from *Parks and Rec* to *It's Always Sunny in Philadelphia*, what you'll find beneath the punchlines is truth. Truth about relationships, insecurities, dreams, failures, hope. Comedy is funny because it's real. Because it exaggerates what we already recognize and plays with it in a way that surprises us. And that's your job now. Not just to write jokes—but to write the **truth**, only funnier.

Here's the good news: the funny stuff is already in you. Whether it's dry wit, slapstick absurdity, ironic commentary, or just pure silliness, your sense of humor is your fuel. This book, and ChatGPT, are just here to help you refine it into something that can live on screen, episode after episode.

ChatGPT works best when it works with *you*. This isn't about hitting a magic button and getting a finished sitcom. This is about having a creative partner who can help you brainstorm characters, punch up dialogue, shape arcs, and help you get unstuck when your brain hits a wall. It's here to mirror your voice, test your ideas, and even throw a few curveballs you didn't see coming. It's your virtual writers' room, your brainstorming buddy, your non-judgmental collaborator who's always awake and never needs a coffee break.

Now, if you're wondering whether you really can write a TV comedy series in just one day, the answer is: yes, **you** can. Not because you'll be perfect on the first draft (nobody is), but because this method focuses on **finishing**, not fussing. By the end of today, you'll have a working pilot, a cast of recurring characters, the world they live in, episode ideas, and a tone that's uniquely yours. That's not just a good day's work—it's a legitimate foundation for a real show.

So, here's what I want you to do: take a deep breath. Shake off the pressure. This isn't school, and you're not being graded. There are no gatekeepers here. Just you, your ideas, and a co-writer that's ready when you are. If you can tap into what makes you laugh, and what you want to say to the world, then you've already got something special brewing. Let's turn that spark into a flame—and that flame into a full-blown TV series.

Ready to write funny on purpose?

Let's go.

Why ChatGPT Is Your New Comedy Writing Partner

Writing comedy can be one of the loneliest creative pursuits. You spend hours staring at a blinking cursor, wondering if your punchline is funny or if your brain is just broken from overwork. You write a joke and instantly second-guess it. Is it too obvious? Too weird? Too dark? Not dark enough? Then you rewrite it, and before long, you've lost the rhythm of the scene and you're questioning your life choices. That's when you realize you don't need another coffee—you need a partner. And that's where ChatGPT steps in.

Now, I know what you might be thinking. "AI? Writing comedy? Isn't that cheating—or worse, soulless?" But let me stop you right there. ChatGPT isn't here to replace your sense of humor. It's here to reflect it, stretch it, test it, and help you turn that spark of an idea into an entire firework show of scenes, characters, and jokes. If you use it right, ChatGPT becomes the co-writer who never argues over credit, never gets jealous of your ideas, and never tells you your favorite joke is "too niche."

Think of ChatGPT as the ultimate brainstorming engine. It's tireless. It's fast. It doesn't get bogged down in perfectionism. If you say, "Give me five different ways a character could fall off a ladder and still make it funny," it'll do exactly that in seconds. You can ask it to write the same joke ten different ways, or turn a dramatic monologue into an absurd comedy rant, or build an entire episode premise around something completely stupid like a dog getting elected mayor—and it'll go with you every step of the way.

But here's the real power of using ChatGPT in comedy writing: it helps you *fail faster*. Comedy is iterative. The first idea is rarely the best one. But with ChatGPT, you can generate ten more ideas in the time it would have taken you to second-guess the first. You're no longer at the mercy of your mood or your energy level. Writer's block loses its power because you always have something to react to, something to push against. You don't have to stare at a blank page—you can start by reacting to what ChatGPT gives you, and in the process, discover where your voice fits.

Another thing ChatGPT does well is character dynamics. You can give it two character types and ask it to generate funny dialogue between them, or throw them into ridiculous situations just to see what comes out. The more detail you give it—personality traits, quirks, emotional hangups—the more specific and surprising the responses will be. Suddenly you're not just writing scenes; you're hearing characters talk in ways that reveal who they really are. That's comedy gold.

And then there's structure. Comedy writing is all about timing, pacing, escalation, and payoff. If you're not sure how to organize your story beats or how to make a subplot echo the main plot in a clever way, ChatGPT can help you plot it out. Want a slow burn that explodes in the final minutes? A string of misunderstandings that all collide in one room? An emotional arc that somehow loops back to a chicken costume? ChatGPT doesn't blink—it just delivers.

You can also train it to match your tone. If your humor tends to be dry and sarcastic, you can tell it that. If you write in a fast-paced, quippy style like *Arrested Development* or *Veep*, ChatGPT can lean into that too. It's a chameleon that responds to your creative direction, and the more you interact with it, the better it becomes at echoing your voice. You're not just using a tool—you're shaping it as you go.

And let's talk speed. Normally, writing a comedy pilot could take weeks of outlining, revising, punching up, and panicking. With ChatGPT, you can go from idea to first draft in a few hours. That doesn't mean it'll be perfect—but it means you'll have something you can work with, build on, and revise. It lets you do the thing so many writers struggle with: actually *finish* something.

One of the smartest ways to use ChatGPT is to let it take the pressure off. You don't have to come up with the perfect line on your own. You don't have to get every joke right the first time. You don't even have to fully understand your own idea yet. You can ask, "What's funny about a character who's allergic to their own emotional growth?" or "Give me a few episode ideas where everything goes wrong at a workplace that makes funeral balloons," and ChatGPT will throw things at you you'd never have come up with alone. That kind of wild associative thinking? It's exactly what great comedy needs.

But don't forget: *you* are the comedian. ChatGPT is the sidekick. You decide what's funny. You choose what feels right for your tone, your show, your audience. It doesn't replace your instincts—it sharpens them. It gives you options you didn't know you had, and it gives you the momentum to keep going when you might otherwise stall.

If you've ever wished for a writer's room in your laptop, that's basically what ChatGPT is. A flexible, fast, idea-spitting partner who won't laugh at their own jokes before you do. And sure, sometimes it will throw out a truly terrible idea, but that's part of the fun. Even bad suggestions can spark great ones. The point is, you're not doing this alone anymore.

So, welcome to your new comedy writing process: you, your ideas, your unique sense of humor—and ChatGPT, ready to make sure the room is never quiet for long.

Let's write something hilarious.

What Is Comedy, Really?

Comedy is one of those things that everyone recognizes but few can truly define. It's more than just telling jokes. It's more than writing funny lines or having your characters fall face-first into wedding cakes. Comedy is a way of seeing the world. It's a reaction to chaos, a survival mechanism, a protest, a mirror, a sigh, and a celebration—all rolled into one weird, laughable moment. If you're going to write a great comedy series, it helps to know what you're actually working with. So let's unpack what comedy really is and why it matters more than we sometimes admit.

At its heart, comedy is about contrast. It plays with opposites: expectation and reality, dignity and embarrassment, truth and exaggeration. When you laugh, it's usually because something happens that breaks the pattern you were prepared for. That's why timing matters. That's why surprise is key. Comedy takes what you think is going to happen and either flips it upside down or dials it up to ridiculous extremes. That moment of dissonance—that tiny explosion of unexpectedness—is where laughter lives.

But it's not just about the unexpected. Comedy also relies on recognition. When we see ourselves in a character, or when a joke hits close to home, the laugh comes with a sense of "yes, that's exactly what life feels like." Comedy isn't always escapism. In many cases, it's a way of dealing with life's difficulties. It helps us talk about awkwardness, pain, and injustice without collapsing under the weight of it all. A great comedy can be both hilarious and heartbreakingly true. Think of *BoJack Horseman*, *The Office*, or *Fleabag*—shows that make you laugh while quietly peeling back the layers of anxiety, self-doubt, or grief.

So if comedy is surprise plus recognition, what's the secret ingredient that makes it work? It's truth. Honest emotion. Honest absurdity. Honest reactions. You can have a wild, ridiculous premise—like two losers running a bar with no customers—but if the characters respond in ways that feel genuine, the comedy lands. The moment you force it, or write something just because it seems "funny," you start to lose the spark. The best laughs don't come from trying too hard—they come from getting it right.

There are lots of tools that comedy writers use to build laughs. There's wordplay, slapstick, irony, sarcasm, misdirection, repetition, exaggeration, and the classic "rule of three." There's the setup and punchline, the comedic callback, the visual gag, the awkward silence. You don't need to master them all right now, but understanding that these are the building blocks will help you shape your style. You might lean into dry wit. Or surrealism. Or physical comedy. Or a steady stream of awkward social encounters. Whatever makes you laugh—that's your compass.

Another thing to know is that comedy always has stakes. They might be emotional, relational, professional, or even existential. But something always matters to someone, even in the silliest situations. The characters want things. They're trying. They're failing. They're holding on to dignity by a thread. And the comedy comes from how their goals crash into each other—or into the absurdity of the world around them. Think about *Curb Your Enthusiasm*. Larry wants simple things—courtesy, logic, fairness—but the world refuses to play along. That clash is the joke.

Comedy also has rhythm. You'll feel it as you write. It's the pace of the dialogue, the timing of the reaction, the beat between the setup and the payoff. Some shows are fast and punchy, others take their time with long setups and unexpected twists. Some lean on dialogue, others on visuals. A moment that plays flat on the page might come alive with the right pacing. When writing your own series, try reading scenes out loud. You'll hear where it drags. You'll feel where the punchline hits too soon or too late. That rhythm—like music—takes time to develop, but it's one of the most rewarding parts of writing funny.

And yes, comedy is subjective. What one person finds hilarious, another might shrug off. That's okay. You're not writing to please everyone. You're writing to find your audience—the people who laugh the way you do, who see the world a little tilted, who get the kind of humor you get. The more specific and authentic your comedy is, the more likely it is to connect with the people it's meant for. So don't chase what's trending. Don't imitate. Just be honest—and be funny in your own voice.

One of the beautiful things about comedy is that it's democratic. Anyone can write something funny. You don't need permission. You don't need a perfect résumé. You just need a point of view and the courage to put it into words. And now, with ChatGPT, you also have a creative partner who can help shape, test, and refine those words until they work. You can toss out ideas, shape scenes, revise moments, and try a hundred punchlines in the time it would've taken to write one. It's like having an entire writing staff in your laptop—without the ego or the coffee budget.

So what is comedy, really? It's the unexpected truth. The joyful pain. The little rebellion against how seriously life wants to be taken. It's how we cope, how we connect, how we remind each other that we're not alone in the madness. And if you can harness that, shape it into characters and scenes, and build a world that captures that rhythm, then congratulations: you're not just writing jokes. You're writing a comedy series.

And we've only just begun. Ready to get serious about being funny?

The Many Flavors of Funny: Exploring Comedy Subgenres

Comedy isn't just one thing. It's not confined to a stand-up routine or a sitcom set in a living room. It's a whole spectrum of voices, tones, rhythms, and styles. There are as many kinds of comedy as there are types of laughter—from the shocked gasp-laugh to the wheezy cackle to the slow-building chuckle that comes long after the punchline. If you're writing a comedy series, it's not just about being funny—it's about knowing *what kind* of funny you're aiming for. Choosing your subgenre shapes everything else: your tone, your characters, your pacing, your plots, and even your audience.

Let's start with the classics: **sitcoms**. These are the backbone of television comedy. Sitcoms—short for situation comedies—are built around a central group of characters in a fixed setting. Think *Friends, The Big Bang Theory, Modern Family*, or *Brooklyn Nine-Nine*. The humor is driven by personalities clashing, characters trying to grow (or refusing to), and the endless comedy of everyday life. Sitcoms often rely on structure: an A-plot, B-plot, and resolution, all while returning to the same emotional baseline by the end. They're character-driven, accessible, and built to run for seasons.

Then there's the **workplace comedy**, a subgenre of the sitcom that deserves its own mention. It's where shows like *The Office, Parks and Recreation*, and *Superstore* thrive. These shows mine humor from forced relationships—people who have to deal with each other every day, whether they like it or not. There's rich comedy in bureaucracy, social dynamics, and awkward meetings. Workplace comedies also often evolve into ensemble pieces, where even background characters get their moment to shine.

Next up: **absurdist comedy**. This is where reality goes sideways, and nothing is quite what it seems. Think *The Mighty Boosh, Rick and Morty*, or *I Think You Should Leave*. In this subgenre, logic takes a backseat and exaggeration runs wild. The comedy is surreal, disorienting, often weird for the sake of being weird—and that's the point. If your sense of humor leans toward the dreamlike or the irrational, this might be your playground. These shows require bold vision and strong visual storytelling, because the unexpected is the star.

On the other end of the spectrum, you have **dramedy**—the comedy-drama hybrid. These are shows that aren't afraid to get serious, even dark, but still find humor in pain, absurdity in sadness. *Fleabag, BoJack Horseman, Barry*, and *Atlanta* live in this territory. They bend the rules, play with structure, and often shift tones within a single episode. Dramedies are often emotionally rich and character-centric, using comedy to deepen the pathos rather than deflect it.

There's also **satire**, where the comedy bites. *Veep, South Park, The Simpsons, Arrested Development*—these shows use humor to critique politics, society, or human nature. Satirical comedies are sharp, often fast-talking, and unafraid to go for the jugular. If you've got strong opinions, a keen eye for hypocrisy, and a knack for turning outrage into punchlines, this might be your lane. Just know that satire walks a fine line—it has to be smarter than what it mocks, or it risks reinforcing the very things it's trying to skewer.

Another flavor is **romantic comedy**—or rom-com for short. While more common in film, this genre has had strong TV outings too, like *Crazy Ex-Girlfriend, You're the Worst*, or *Man Seeking Woman*. These shows explore relationships, dating, heartbreak, and awkward flirtation with a comedic lens. They're full of emotional stakes, relatable vulnerabilities, and endless opportunities for miscommunication-based hilarity. They're also fertile ground for character arcs and slow-burn storytelling.

Let's not forget **dark comedy**, where the humor comes from tragedy, discomfort, or taboo subjects. Shows like *The End of the F***ing World**, *Dead to Me*, or *It's Always Sunny in Philadelphia* dive into ethically murky waters and come up laughing. Dark comedies challenge audiences to laugh at what they "shouldn't." They explore flawed characters, moral gray zones, and human absurdity at its bleakest. Writing dark comedy means being fearless—but also responsible. The key is knowing your audience and the line between edgy and cruel.

There's also **family comedy**, which overlaps with the sitcom world but often centers around generational dynamics, parenting, childhood, and domestic chaos. Think *Malcolm in the Middle*, *Black-ish*, *Schitt's Creek*, or *Full House*. These shows have built-in emotional stakes and a warm undercurrent, even when the jokes are edgy. They often aim for a balance of laugh-out-loud and feel-good. If you like to mine humor from everyday life and complicated love, this subgenre gives you plenty to work with.

For fans of big laughs and fast setups, there's **sketch comedy**. This is more fragmented and often more visual, with each scene or bit acting like a self-contained short. *Key & Peele*, *SNL*, *Portlandia*, and *A Black Lady Sketch Show* fall into this category. These series can parody, satirize, go full absurdist, or dabble in all of it. You can use ChatGPT to brainstorm characters and concepts for sketches endlessly—this is the most idea-hungry format of all, and it benefits from high turnover and constant reinvention.

You can also blend genres to create something uniquely yours. *Scrubs* is a medical dramedy. *Community* is a meta-sitcom that jumps between genres week to week. *The Good Place* starts as a philosophical farce and becomes a cosmic drama. *Ted Lasso* is a sports workplace rom-com dramedy. Comedy isn't about staying in a lane—it's about figuring out which lanes help your voice drive best.

So, what flavor speaks to you? What kind of stories do you want to tell—and how do you want your audience to feel when they laugh? That's the real decision. The subgenre isn't just a label—it's your lens. It shapes the world your characters live in, the tone your jokes ride on, and the kind of audience that will tune in week after week. You don't have to pick just one—you can mix and match. But clarity helps. Knowing what kind of funny you're writing makes the rest of the process smoother, from character creation to episode planning to punchline delivery.

And now that you know the flavors of funny, it's time to cook up your own recipe.

Let's build your comedy world.

Sitcom, Dramedy, Sketch, or Surreal? Picking Your Format

Choosing the right format for your comedy series is a little like choosing the right shoes for a journey. If you grab the wrong pair, you'll still make progress, but it'll be clunky, uncomfortable, and you'll probably trip over your own narrative by episode three. The format you choose isn't just a matter of style—it's the backbone of how your story gets told, how jokes land, how arcs develop, and how characters grow or resist growth. It's also the foundation on which ChatGPT can build something cohesive, fast, and funny. So how do you pick the right one?

Start by asking yourself what kind of story you want to tell and how long you want to stay with your characters. If you've got a strong central premise, a recurring group dynamic, and a desire to explore character interactions over time, then the **sitcom** is your go-to. It's built for longevity. It's built for rhythm. Think *Seinfeld*, *Friends*, *Brooklyn Nine-Nine*, or *Superstore*. The sitcom offers a reliable, flexible structure that thrives on character interplay and steady backdrops. You return to the same setting, the same conflicts, and the same lovable dysfunction. It's the genre of comfort and chaos in equal measure.

Sitcoms are great for writers who love writing relationships, comebacks, and running gags. They also work beautifully with ChatGPT, because you can define your characters clearly and then ask the AI to generate entire conversations based on their unique personalities and dynamics. The regular structure—setup, complication, resolution—gives you a framework that's repeatable but never stale. Once you lock in that voice, you'll find yourself churning out episodes with surprising speed and confidence.

But maybe you're not looking to keep it light. Maybe your comedy has teeth, or bruises. Maybe it makes people cry a little while they laugh. Enter the **dramedy**. These half-hour or hour-long series blur the lines between funny and heavy. *Fleabag*, *Atlanta*, *BoJack Horseman*, *Ted Lasso*, and *Barry* have all redefined what a comedy series can be. They deal with death, addiction, loneliness, ambition, guilt—serious things—but they do it with wit, irony, and heart.

If your idea comes from a place of emotional truth, if your characters are more than caricatures, and if the laughter often sneaks up behind something painful, you might be in dramedy territory. Writing this kind of show with ChatGPT means tapping into tone. You can prompt the AI to balance emotional beats with clever dialogue, or have it take a serious scene and sneak in a moment of absurdity. The power of dramedy lies in its ability to be real and ridiculous at the same time.

Now let's swing to the other extreme: **sketch comedy**. This format thrives on brevity, surprise, and sheer volume. It's not about one story—it's about many. *Key & Peele*, *I Think You Should Leave*, *SNL*, and *A Black Lady Sketch Show* are built from rapid-fire setups and punchlines. There's no long arc, no deep character development—just concept after concept, gag after gag.

Sketch is a great format if your mind jumps from idea to idea. It's for writers who want to explore everything from social satire to visual absurdity to out-of-left-field weirdness. With ChatGPT, sketch writing becomes a playground. You can ask for three sketches about time-traveling baristas, or a parody of gritty reboots of nursery rhymes, and it'll throw out a range of ideas faster than a whiteboard in a writer's room. You don't have to build a world—you just have to build a moment. But it means constantly inventing new premises, and that takes stamina.

Then there's **surreal or experimental comedy**, where the structure itself can break. These shows push boundaries and often rewrite the rules of what a series even is. *Rick and Morty*, *The Eric Andre Show*, *Man Seeking Woman*, or *Toast of*

London take traditional formats and twist them into something unpredictable. If your mind goes toward metaphysics, dream logic, or the grotesque, this might be your zone.

Surreal comedy works best when you have a strong creative vision. It requires consistency in its inconsistency. Audiences will go along for the ride if you establish the rules of your weird universe early—and then play with them creatively. ChatGPT can help you brainstorm alternate realities, weird logic, or genre-smashing scenes. You can prompt it to imagine what happens if gravity randomly turns off mid-conversation, or what a therapy session between a dragon and a telepathic plant might look like. The key here is committing to the madness.

Each format has its own storytelling demands and strengths. Sitcoms are character machines. Dramedies are emotional engines. Sketch shows are bursts of fireworks. Surreal comedies are roller coasters with no track. What makes a format right for you is how well it matches your sensibility. Are you interested in evolving character arcs or punchy, high-concept jokes? Do you want to write a single world or build a hundred? Do you want to ground your humor in truth, or launch it into orbit?

Also consider the pace you want to keep. Sitcoms and dramedies benefit from rhythm and long-term planning. Sketch shows demand constant invention. Surreal series test your flexibility and imagination. None are "easier" than the others—but they each suit different creative rhythms. ChatGPT can match any of them. It can help you build tight story structures, rapid-fire sketches, emotionally layered dialogue, or absolutely bonkers set-pieces.

So before you go any further, plant your flag. Decide what type of funny you want to build. Are you writing something that could live on prime time? Or something that belongs in a streaming niche full of cult followers? This decision sets the course for everything that follows: how you develop your characters, how you shape your episodes, and how your comedy finds its heartbeat.

The good news is—you don't have to marry one format forever. You can experiment. You can blend. You can start in one genre and subvert it entirely by episode four. The goal right now is to find the shape that best fits your idea. Once you do that, the writing becomes smoother, more intuitive—and a lot more fun.

So. Sitcom, dramedy, sketch, or surreal?

Pick your format, and let's make it hilarious.

Starting from the End: The Last Laugh Comes First

It might sound backward, but in comedy—as in life—knowing how things end helps you understand what you're really building toward. Most writers start with the beginning. They ask, "What's the premise?" or "Who are the characters?" But in this book, you're going to flip that around. Because in a great comedy series, the *last laugh*—the final moment, the closing image, the ultimate joke or truth—can shape the entire structure, tone, and emotional payoff of the show. You're not just writing scenes to be funny. You're writing a journey that leads to a particular kind of laugh. The kind that resonates. The kind that lingers. The kind that says, "We earned this."

So, what kind of ending do you want?

Is it bittersweet? Is it absurd? Is it a punchline ten seasons in the making? Maybe your characters finally grow up, or finally implode, or maybe nothing changes at all—and that *is* the joke. Maybe your finale leaves the audience laughing through tears, or stunned into silence by a final meta twist. Whatever tone you're going for—sincere, cynical, chaotic, redemptive—defining it now gives your series a target. It's not about spoilers; it's about structure.

Let's break this down with examples. *The Good Place* ends not with a gag, but with a quiet moment of spiritual peace—and the show builds toward that idea from episode one, even if it doesn't seem like it at first. *Seinfeld*, on the other hand, ends with all four characters in jail, trapped in their own selfish loop. *The Office* closes on a wedding and a sense of nostalgic completion. *BoJack Horseman* fades out on a rooftop conversation that's funny, awkward, and haunting all at once. These endings don't just conclude a story—they fulfill the *point* of the story.

By starting from your ending, you're giving yourself clarity. You're answering the question: *What is this series really about?* Because comedy isn't just about being funny. It's about saying something true in a way people can laugh about. And if you can articulate what your last laugh means, then you can start designing every earlier episode to build up to it—through jokes, character arcs, reversals, and emotional beats.

So let's use ChatGPT to explore your ending. Try feeding it prompts like:

- "Give me three different possible series finales for a comedy about two failed magicians trying to make a comeback."
- "Describe a last scene for a dramedy where the main character has been lying about their identity for years."
- "What's a satisfying yet ironic ending to a workplace comedy set in a call center for angry pets?"

You don't have to pick the first idea. In fact, try ten. Try twenty. Let the possibilities bounce around. You'll know when one hits right—when it feels like a laugh that comes not just from a joke, but from the entire journey.

Once you have that final laugh in your head, everything changes. Suddenly, your character arcs become clearer. You know where each of them ends up, which means you can trace their steps backward. Who were they in episode one? How far have they come—or not come? What patterns did they break, or fall deeper into? Did their love story pan out? Did they ruin everything beautifully? Are they better? Worse? Just... older?

And you don't have to save all the best stuff for the end. You can build in echoes—mini versions of your final moment that appear earlier in the season. Setups that foreshadow the finale. Running gags that pay off in unexpected, cathartic ways. If your series ends with a major reversal—say, the slacker becomes the CEO—you can start planting the seeds early. Use ChatGPT to help brainstorm the slow transformations. Ask it how a character like yours could evolve—or fake growth just convincingly enough to get a laugh when they blow it at the last second.

Now, what about tone? Because your ending also determines your emotional ceiling. If you want to close on a serious note, you need to lay groundwork throughout the show that allows for depth. If you want to close on a massive, ridiculous twist, then you're building a tone that allows absurdity to escalate. Either way, the finale informs the rules of your world. It tells you what's possible.

And if you're writing a show you hope will go on for multiple seasons, don't worry—you can still start from the end. Just pick the end of *season one*. Or even the end of your *pilot*. Ask: what is the final image of this episode? What's the closing beat? Is it a laugh that undercuts everything that came before? A romantic twist? A sudden reveal that throws the whole setup into question? Knowing that moment gives your episode shape. You're aiming at something. You're writing *toward* something.

It's the difference between wandering through jokes and building to a punchline. And in comedy, timing is everything.

The beauty of working with ChatGPT is that once you've chosen your ending, you can reverse-engineer everything that leads up to it. Ask it to map out key turning points. Ask it how to shift your character's perspective one step at a time. Ask it for plot ideas that slowly circle around the theme of your final moment. The AI becomes your architect, helping you scaffold each layer so that when you hit that last laugh, it feels earned.

So, what's your final moment? What's the tone? The joke? The truth under the joke?

Once you know that, you're not just writing a comedy series—you're *finishing* one. And that's where the magic really starts.

Let's build backward, one laugh at a time.

Reverse Engineering Your Comedy Series

If you've ever tried to build a piece of Ikea furniture without looking at the finished picture on the box, you know how chaotic and demoralizing it can be. Writing a comedy series is no different—except the screws are your plot points and the instruction manual is whatever structure you invent (or ignore). That's why reverse engineering is such a powerful approach. You start with the picture on the box—the final moment, the last laugh, the emotional payoff—and then work backward to figure out how to get there. It's a method that gives your series a strong backbone, whether you're writing twenty-minute sitcom episodes, a dramedy with long arcs, or something weird and sketch-based.

In the last chapter, you imagined your final moment. Maybe it was an ironic twist, a character's epiphany, or a big comedic payoff that tied all your themes together. Great. That's your destination. Now you need to figure out what needs to happen to make that moment *matter*. That's where reverse engineering comes in. This is where you pull the thread backward and ask: *How did we get here?*

Let's say your comedy series ends with your main character quitting their dead-end job and finally taking a leap into their dream career. Simple enough, but what gives that moment weight? Maybe they've failed to do so five times before. Maybe they were sabotaged by their best friend in episode six. Maybe they lied on their résumé in episode two and got called out in episode nine. Each of those moments becomes a stepping stone that leads to the final act. You're not randomly building a story—you're tracing the path of a narrative you already understand in hindsight.

Now let's apply this to structure. A typical comedy season—especially in sitcoms or dramedies—runs about eight to twelve episodes. That gives you plenty of space to develop arcs, weave running gags, and escalate absurdity. When reverse engineering, start by identifying your season's endpoint, then ask what needs to shift for each major character to reach that point. For each shift, you now have the seeds of an episode.

ChatGPT can help immensely here. You can tell it your end goal and ask, "What kind of episode would set this up three chapters earlier?" or "What's a situation that would force this character to confront their fear of change in a funny way?" If you've already built out your characters, ask ChatGPT to walk through a beat-by-beat breakdown of how they evolve—or resist evolution—across the season. You'll get a chain of events that actually leads somewhere instead of just looping endlessly around the same joke.

Reverse engineering also applies to jokes themselves. The best comedy often comes from setup and payoff. When you know the punchline you want, you can go back and ask, "How do I set this up in a way that feels invisible at first, but inevitable in hindsight?" That's where callbacks become comedy gold. A throwaway line in episode one can become the gut-busting closer in episode ten. ChatGPT can suggest different ways to plant jokes early, using subtle dialogue, visual gags, or recurring motifs.

You can also use reverse engineering to build emotional arcs. Say your show ends on a reconciled friendship. You can trace the fallout backward—what broke them apart? What caused the rift? What forced them to choose sides? Once you've mapped the deterioration, you can layer each episode with clues, tension, and missed opportunities for reconnection, so the final reunion becomes more than just sweet—it becomes earned.

And don't stop at just one ending. Try several. Give ChatGPT different endings and ask how the journey would look if you went with each one. If your comedy ends with a romantic pairing, it's a different show than if it ends with an epic failure or an alien invasion. The shape of the arc changes. The types of jokes shift. The tone adapts. By trying out multiple conclusions, you'll discover what kind of story you're *really* telling.

Reverse engineering also helps you avoid filler. If you know what you're building toward, you won't write episodes that meander or repeat the same beats. You'll have clear progressions. You'll know what each episode needs to accomplish—what emotional or comedic beat it needs to land—so you can craft tight, purposeful stories.

For sketch comedy or absurdist formats, reverse engineering still applies. Think of a sketch show as a symphony of small endings. Each sketch has a punchline, a twist, a surprise exit. If you know what that punchline is, you can ask ChatGPT to help brainstorm the wildest way to get there. "If the joke is that the therapist turns out to be a houseplant, what's the most serious buildup I can write to make that reveal land harder?" Let the destination dictate the rhythm.

In the end, reverse engineering is less about control and more about clarity. Comedy might look chaotic on the surface, but underneath the laughs is an incredibly precise machine. Timing matters. Pacing matters. Emotional logic matters. And when you start with the end, you can sculpt all those details with confidence.

So instead of wandering into your story with nothing but vibes and a funny character voice, walk in with a map. Know what your final laugh is. Then challenge yourself to build a path where every joke, every setback, every interaction points toward that moment—even if your characters have no idea what's coming.

Your audience will feel it. They'll sense the build-up. And when the moment hits, it won't just be funny—it'll be unforgettable.

Time to write backward so your comedy can move forward.

Generating a Comedy Concept That Sticks

Every great comedy series starts with one deceptively simple thing: the concept. The "what if" idea that forms the spine of everything that follows. *What if a group of nerds struggled to function in the real world?* (*The Big Bang Theory*). *What if a documentary crew followed office workers who barely tolerated each other?* (*The Office*). *What if a sweet, clueless coach was hired to run a soccer team in a foreign country?* (*Ted Lasso*). These ideas are clear, bold, and most importantly—they stick. They give writers room to play, evolve, and build stories for seasons. Your job now is to find your own.

But first, let's get one thing straight: a sticky comedy concept doesn't have to be outrageous. It just has to have tension. It needs conflict baked in. It needs a strong central irony. It needs a situation or world that throws your characters off balance and keeps them there. The best concepts aren't safe—they're a little risky, a little broken, a little weird. They ask a question that the series then tries to answer, over and over, in slightly different ways.

This is where ChatGPT becomes your brainstorming engine. If you feed it the right prompts, it'll throw more concepts at you than a whole table of sleep-deprived comedy writers. Start with simple inputs like:

- "Give me ten funny show ideas involving unlikely roommates."
- "What's a unique workplace I could set a sitcom in?"
- "Pitch me some absurd but emotionally grounded comedy premises."

You'll start seeing the edges of something interesting. Maybe it's a goat herder who becomes a tech CEO overnight. Or a ghost who's stuck haunting a tiny apartment with three clueless influencers. Or an adult child trying to run a failing amusement park with their estranged parents. Even the ones that don't quite hit can lead you to something that does.

Once you've got a few solid contenders, the next step is to test for **stickiness**. A sticky concept has three key traits: it's simple, it's loaded with tension, and it's built for repeatability.

Simple doesn't mean basic. It means you can pitch it in one sentence. *What if vampires ran a share house in the suburbs?* That's *What We Do in the Shadows*. It immediately invites comedy. If you can't summarize your concept without needing five paragraphs of backstory, it's not ready. Try this test: could someone describe it quickly to a friend and make them laugh or get curious? If yes—you're close.

Tension is the engine of comedy. Opposites colliding. People trying to hide things. Flaws that are constantly exposed. A sticky concept throws your characters into situations where they're out of their depth. Think *Arrested Development*—a responsible man trying to keep a wildly dysfunctional family together. That tension drives every single joke. So, ask yourself: what's the built-in conflict? What will make your characters constantly crash into each other and the world around them?

Repeatability is your long game. You need a concept that generates stories. Over and over. Can your idea sustain 10–12 episodes a season, maybe for several seasons? Does the world you've created offer fresh situations, secondary characters, places to go, relationships to explore, and new complications? If the answer is no, it might be a great short film, but not a series. Use ChatGPT to stress-test your concept. Prompt it with, "Give me a list of possible episode plots for a comedy about..." and see how many unique situations it can generate. If the list runs dry after five, you may need to expand the world or rethink the hook.

Here's another trick: take a familiar format and twist it. What's a version of *The Office*, but set in a failing pirate ship? What's a version of *Friends*, but they're all in witness protection and living under aliases? That kind of genre-bending or setting-flipping can make a familiar concept feel totally fresh.

And don't be afraid to go personal. Many of the best comedy concepts come from a sliver of truth—a job you hated, a bizarre neighbor, a family situation too ridiculous to make up. Comedy comes alive when the idea feels grounded in something real, even if the world around it is exaggerated. If you use ChatGPT to help dig into your own experiences, you can turn "my dad once tried to build a panic room out of pool noodles" into an entire show about doomsday preppers who don't actually know what they're doing.

Once you've found a concept that sticks with you—something that still makes you smile ten minutes after you thought of it—you've got your foundation. That's the seed your characters, themes, tone, and arcs will all grow from. The rest of the writing process becomes easier because the concept itself keeps giving you material. You won't have to force ideas—they'll come naturally from the premise.

Let your comedy concept be specific, weird, meaningful, and a little risky. If it makes you laugh and makes someone else ask, "Wait, what happens next?"—you've got something real.

Ready to build the world around that idea?

Let's keep going.

Building a Show Premise That's Both Funny and Flexible

So, you've landed on a comedy concept that makes you laugh. That's a huge step. Now it's time to turn that spark into a *premise*—the central engine of your show. The premise is the DNA of your series. It's not just "what the show is about." It's the structure, the expectation, and the reason audiences will keep coming back. A strong premise doesn't just set the tone for one episode—it opens the door to an entire universe of stories, jokes, and moments. And if you're building your show with ChatGPT, the premise is also the key input that will keep generating ideas that make sense in your world.

But here's the challenge: your premise has to be both funny and *flexible*. Funny, because, well, it's comedy. But flexible, because you're going to be writing this thing over multiple episodes, maybe multiple seasons. The biggest mistake comedy writers make is confusing a sketch idea for a series. A one-joke world might kill in a three-minute short, but if it can't grow, evolve, and surprise, it's going to burn out by episode three. Flexibility is what turns a funny idea into a funny *show*.

Let's start by clarifying what a premise really is. It's not a tagline. It's not a slogan. It's not the logline you'd pitch in an elevator. Your premise is the ongoing conflict that drives every episode. It usually involves characters who are stuck in a situation that creates friction, pressure, or contradiction. They want things they can't quite get. They deal with people they can't escape. They live in a world that constantly undermines their plans. That tension fuels the humor and the plot.

Take *The Office*: the premise isn't just "people work in an office." It's that a group of ordinary employees must endure the bizarre leadership of a man who sees himself as a comedic genius and life coach. The friction between that delusion and the drudgery of office life *is* the show. Every episode flows from that premise.

Or *Schitt's Creek*: "A wealthy family loses everything and has to live in a town they once bought as a joke." That's not just a funny setup—it's a premise that allows for endless situations involving class tension, emotional growth, and personality clashes.

To build your own funny and flexible premise, ask yourself a few core questions:

- Who are the characters?
- What is their *shared situation*?
- Why can't they easily leave or change it?
- What emotional or situational pressure keeps the tension alive?
- What kind of humor naturally arises from that pressure?

Now, turn to ChatGPT. Describe the concept you've got so far and ask it:

"Expand this into a comedy show premise that allows for multiple storylines, character arcs, and different comedic situations."

Or:

"What complications can keep this situation fresh over a season?"

You can also test your premise by running it through a few "what if" scenarios. Ask:

- "What would a holiday episode look like in this show?"

- "What happens when a character tries to leave this situation?"
- "Can this premise support a slow-burn romance, a rivalry, a betrayal, a guest star?"

If your show still works—and stays funny—when you imagine these scenarios, you're onto something with staying power.

Here's a trick that often helps: imagine your show at three different scales. First, what's the *pilot* episode? Then, what's an episode from *season two*? And finally, what does the *series finale* look like? If the characters and conflict can evolve while still staying true to the core tension, then your premise has depth. You're not writing the same joke every week—you're watching people navigate a world that keeps challenging them.

You can also try the "genre flip" test with ChatGPT. Take your premise and say, "Reimagine this as a romantic comedy," or "What if this were a murder mystery with the same setup?" If the characters still feel alive in that world—even when the genre shifts—you've created a flexible foundation. That flexibility gives you room to grow, twist, and surprise your audience while staying rooted in your central idea.

Your premise should also be generous. That means it should generate secondary characters, new subplots, and running gags almost effortlessly. For example, if your show is about two underqualified people running a failing zoo, then you've got room for episodes about animal escapes, PR disasters, eccentric visitors, and municipal inspectors. You don't have to invent new worlds every week—the premise opens up the sandbox and gives you tools to play.

And finally, your premise should have a soul. Even the silliest comedies work best when they're about something. *Community* is about the need for belonging. *BoJack Horseman* is about self-destruction and recovery. *Ted Lasso* is about optimism and emotional intelligence in the face of cynicism. That underlying truth doesn't need to be loud or preachy—it just needs to exist. Ask yourself: what emotional engine runs underneath the jokes? If you can feel it, your audience will too.

So here's your mission now: take that idea that made you laugh, and shape it into something that can hold an entire world. Use ChatGPT to test, stretch, and twist it until it reveals not just its surface joke, but its deeper potential. When the setup, conflict, characters, and tone all align—and you can imagine yourself writing the tenth episode as easily as the first—you've got a premise that's ready to go the distance.

Creating Your Comedy Series Bible in a Day

If the pilot is your show's opening number, the series bible is the full score. It's your guidebook, your pitch deck, your creative manifesto—and it's the thing that proves you've thought this comedy through beyond just a few funny scenes. It doesn't have to be long, it doesn't have to be formal, but it *does* have to be clear, confident, and full of potential. If someone asked you, "What's your show?" your series bible is the best possible answer, all written out and ready to impress. And yes, with ChatGPT's help, you really can write it in a single day.

So what goes into a comedy series bible? It's part story engine, part blueprint, and part invitation. It tells the reader (or you, if you're building as you go) what this show is, who it's about, why it's funny, where it's set, what kind of stories it tells, and how it can evolve. It shows that you understand your own tone and can sustain it over time. And it's not just for producers or networks—it's for you. This document becomes your creative compass. When you're stuck on episode twelve, it's your reminder of what the show was always meant to be.

Here's what we're going to build today using ChatGPT:

Start with **the show's title and tagline**. It doesn't have to be perfect, but it should capture the tone and theme. Think *Arrested Development, The Good Place, Unbreakable Kimmy Schmidt*—the name often does some heavy lifting, so try a few. Ask ChatGPT:

"Give me 10 potential titles for a workplace comedy about failed inventors living in a garage lab."

Or:

"What's a catchy title for a dramedy about a dog walker who also helps clients fix their relationships?"

Once you've landed on something you like, add a **logline**—a one- or two-sentence summary that explains the core of the show. This is your elevator pitch. A great logline includes the setup, the main character(s), the conflict, and the tone. Think: *"A disgraced children's author fakes being a therapist and accidentally becomes a life coach to the emotionally unstable."*

Then comes **the premise paragraph**. This is your "What is the show?" moment. It should explain the central idea, the tone, and why this world keeps generating stories. Use ChatGPT to expand your logline into a full paragraph. Prompt it with:

"Turn this one-sentence premise into a paragraph that explains the tone, story engine, and character relationships."

Next up: **character breakdowns**. List your core cast—usually four to six characters is a good range to start—and describe each one in a paragraph. Go beyond just quirks. Describe what they want, what holds them back, and how they create or collide with comedy. For each, you can ask ChatGPT:

"Describe a funny, emotionally layered character who's the overqualified assistant to a clueless boss,"

or

"Create a comedic foil to this character: a lazy genius who accidentally solves everyone's problems."

Then, create **the world of the show**. Where does it take place? Why is it funny? What are the "rules" of the world? Is it grounded and realistic, or heightened and absurd? Is it set in one location like a bar, a café, a family home—or does it move around? This section is about tone and setting. If it's a town, what kind of town? If it's a workplace, who else works there? Ask ChatGPT to generate ideas for odd locations, supporting characters, and recurring places that can fuel stories. The more specific, the better.

After that, write **sample episode summaries**. Start with your pilot—what happens, how the characters are introduced, and how the series hook is established. Then come up with 4 to 6 additional episodes that reflect what the show can do. Don't just list them—explain the core conflict of each episode and what changes by the end. Ask ChatGPT:

"Give me five episode ideas for a sitcom about a scam self-help guru faking enlightenment."

These summaries show how your show sustains itself over time and give a sense of range—some emotional, some ridiculous, some plot-driven, some character-based.

Include **themes and tone**. This section tells the reader (and reminds you) what your show is really *about* beneath the jokes. It could be about failure, reinvention, friendship, deception, love, regret, ambition—whatever lives under the comedy. Also talk about the kind of humor. Is it fast-paced and dialogue-heavy? Visual and physical? Awkward and subtle? Surreal and strange? Grounded in truth or built on absurdity?

Now add a short note on **the season arc**. What changes by the end of season one? Does a relationship shift? Does someone's secret come out? Does a dynamic flip? Even if the show is largely episodic, there's usually some evolution or progression that gives the season shape.

You can also include **influences**—other shows or creators you admire whose tone or approach might be similar. This isn't copying; it's placing your show in context. If your show is *The Office* meets *Russian Doll*, say so. It gives people a sense of what to expect and how to read your humor.

Wrap it all up with a **final note** about your vision. Why this show, why now, why you? It doesn't have to be personal, but it should be authentic. What makes this comedy matter to you? What do you want people to feel—besides entertained—when they watch it?

Now take all of this, use ChatGPT to refine each section, format it cleanly, and by the end of the day, you'll be holding your own series bible—a living document you can use to pitch, plan, write, and stay focused. You'll know what the show is, what it can become, and how every piece connects to the next.

This isn't just paperwork—it's proof that your idea has legs.

And now that you've got your bible, let's move on to the pilot. Time to bring it to life.

The Pilot Episode: Where It All Begins

If your comedy series were a band, the pilot episode would be the debut single—the track that introduces your sound, hooks your audience, and gets them humming the tune for the rest of the album. The pilot is where it all begins, and it carries a bigger load than any other episode. It doesn't just have to be funny—it has to introduce characters, establish the world, launch the series conflict, set the tone, hint at long-term arcs, and still deliver laughs. It's a balancing act, and it's what separates a clever idea from a real, living show.

A great pilot doesn't just open the door—it sets the pace for everything that comes next. It should feel like a mini version of your entire series. Not a trailer or a teaser, but a full, self-contained story that shows exactly what kind of ride we're in for. It should make viewers want episode two—not just because of what happens next, but because they now trust the world you've built. They want more of *this*.

Start by returning to your series bible. What's the core premise? Who are the key characters? What's the central conflict? Now ask: how can you dramatize all of that in 22–30 minutes? That doesn't mean info-dumping everything at once. It means carefully choosing which moments to show and which ones to hint at. It means showing your characters in action, not giving long introductions. Let the story tell us who they are.

A common and effective approach is the **"disruption model."** Begin with the world as it normally functions—then introduce a change that kicks the series into motion. That change could be a new hire, a breakup, a lawsuit, a death, a scam, a surprise inheritance—anything that shakes up the status quo and forces the characters into new dynamics. This disruption becomes the narrative engine of the pilot and often sets up the entire series arc. Ask ChatGPT for help by prompting:

"Give me five disruption-based pilot ideas for a show about retired bank robbers trying to go straight."

Your pilot also needs to deliver your show's first major laughs—but those laughs should come from *character and conflict*, not just gags. If you've built strong characters in your series bible, you can now ask ChatGPT to write dialogue or scenes where those characters clash. Prompt it with something like:

"Write a short dialogue scene between an uptight wedding planner and her chaos-loving assistant as they prep for a funeral by mistake."

These character-based moments are where the real comedy lives.

Next, consider structure. Most pilots follow a three-act format even if they're just 22 minutes long. You want to open with your hook, then escalate conflict, then resolve or reframe that conflict in a way that reveals something deeper about the characters. If it's a sitcom, you might end on a laugh that restores the world to its wobbly balance. If it's a dramedy, you might let the emotion linger beneath the final joke.

Think about **stakes**. They don't have to be life-or-death, but they should matter deeply to the characters. Maybe the slacker really doesn't want to lose his part-time job because it's his only anchor to reality. Maybe the overly confident guru doesn't want to be exposed as a fraud because it would ruin the fantasy he's built for himself. Stakes create tension. Tension creates comedy. Ask ChatGPT to help with character-based stakes:

"What's at stake emotionally for a character who pretends to be an expert but knows nothing?"

Once you've got your premise, structure, and conflict mapped out, turn to the visual side. What are the most iconic, strange, or memorable images in your pilot? Can you open with something that makes people lean in immediately? A nun on roller skates robbing a bank? A dog giving a TED Talk? A man proposing to the wrong person in front of 400 people? Visual hooks matter. The first 30 seconds of your pilot are your handshake with the audience. Ask ChatGPT:

"Give me five visual cold open ideas for a comedy about college professors with no credentials."

Now look at how the episode ends. Does it deliver a resolution that satisfies the story but leaves something unfinished? Can you hint at what the season might explore without giving it all away? Maybe there's a twist, a reveal, or just a hilarious complication. Maybe the character thinks they've solved their problem—but they've only made it worse. That's your invitation to episode two.

Throughout this process, keep returning to your **tone**. Your pilot isn't just introducing what happens—it's showing *how* it happens. Is the humor dry? Slapstick? Verbal? Surreal? Satirical? Make sure the writing reflects that from the start. Use ChatGPT to help you refine the tone by rewriting a scene in different comedic voices:

"Rewrite this scene in the style of *Arrested Development*,"

or

"Make this interaction funnier with deadpan humor and understated reactions."

Finally, keep it **tight**. A pilot should feel brisk and intentional. It doesn't have time to wander or stall. If a character, line, or subplot doesn't contribute to either laughs or story momentum, cut it. The goal isn't to show everything—it's to show *enough* to prove there's a whole world worth exploring.

So write the episode. Let ChatGPT help you test scenes, punch up jokes, shape character dynamics, and revise dialogue. Read it out loud. Feel the rhythm. Tweak what doesn't land. And when it finally clicks, you'll know you've not only started your comedy series—you've launched something that could go the distance.

This is where it begins.

Now let's write the rest of the season.

How to Structure a Comedy Pilot Script

You've got your characters. You've built your world. You know the premise and even mapped out your pilot episode. Now comes the part where your idea becomes real: the script. A comedy pilot script is your first true test as a series creator. It's not just a proof of concept—it's your story's heartbeat. It's where we meet your characters for the first time, get a feel for your tone, laugh at your jokes, and start to care about people we just met a few minutes ago. And all of that has to happen in roughly 22–30 pages. No pressure, right?

Here's the good news: structure is your best friend. A great pilot follows a structure that gives it flow, rhythm, and clarity. This doesn't mean it has to feel rigid. In fact, the more comfortable you are with structure, the more freely you can break it when the story calls for it. Comedy pilots—especially those for half-hour formats—usually follow a three-act structure with optional cold open and tag scenes. Think of it as setup, escalation, and payoff.

Let's break it down so you can build yours today—with a little help from ChatGPT along the way.

Cold Open (Optional, But Powerful)

This is your first chance to grab attention. It's a quick scene—sometimes even just 30 seconds—that delivers a laugh, a surprise, or a moment of absurdity that sets the tone. It doesn't have to tie into the plot right away, but it should reflect your show's energy. A cold open can be a character doing something ridiculous, a visual gag, a fake-out, or an awkward exchange.

Ask ChatGPT:

"Give me a cold open for a comedy about a family of scam artists trying to act normal at PTA meetings."

Act One – The Setup

This is where we meet your characters and see their world in its default state. Who are they? What's their normal? Show us their flaws, their dynamic, and the tone of their world. Then—most importantly—introduce the **inciting incident**. This is the disruption that shakes things up and sets the story in motion. Maybe a new boss arrives. Maybe someone gets fired. Maybe there's a big misunderstanding or a strange delivery. Whatever it is, it should create tension or a problem that the characters must deal with in a way that reflects who they are.

Ask ChatGPT:

"What would be a strong inciting incident for a pilot about three former reality stars forced to live in one apartment?"

Act Two – Escalation and Complications

Now the characters are reacting. The stakes are rising (even if those stakes are petty or ridiculous). Misunderstandings deepen. Plans go sideways. Relationships get tested. This is where your subplots can start to take shape if you're using an A/B structure. Usually, the main plot gets about two-thirds of the screen time, while a smaller subplot gives you extra laughs and world-building.

Keep in mind that Act Two is where most scripts sag if the conflict isn't clear. Each scene should move something forward. If your characters aren't actively trying to solve the problem—or making it worse—then it's just filler.

Ask ChatGPT to help you brainstorm middle beats:

"What are three complications that could arise if a character lies on their first day at work and tries to keep it going?"

Act Three – Payoff and Resolution

This is where things come to a head. The lie gets exposed. The secret comes out. The weird scheme backfires. Something shifts. Maybe it's a temporary resolution, or maybe the characters learn *just enough* to suggest growth (before reverting back to their original state next week). Your ending should feel earned, and ideally, it should echo the theme of the episode. If it ends with a joke—and it should—it needs to be your best one. Leave us laughing and wanting more.

You can also add a **tag scene**—a final mini-scene after the credits or just before fade-out that delivers one last joke or twist. These often pay off a subplot or callback. Ask ChatGPT:

"Give me three tag scene ideas for a comedy about a struggling startup run by total idiots."

Timing and Pacing

A half-hour comedy script usually runs between 22 and 30 pages, depending on whether it's being written for broadcast (with commercials) or streaming. That means every page counts. Comedy thrives on rhythm—short scenes, snappy dialogue, fast transitions. If a scene starts to drag, it's time to cut, compress, or rewrite. You're not here to explain—you're here to show and make it funny.

Use ChatGPT to test pacing by asking:

"Condense this two-page dialogue into something punchier while keeping the characters' voices distinct."

Or:

"Rewrite this emotional scene with a touch of absurd humor that fits the tone."

Formatting Matters

Comedy scripts follow industry-standard formatting. Character names are centered and capitalized. Dialogue is double-spaced beneath the character name. Action lines are short and visual. Parentheticals are used sparingly. Scene headings (INT./EXT., LOCATION, TIME) are clear and consistent. If you're not sure, you can upload an example and ask ChatGPT to match the format—or use it to reformat scenes you've written in plain text.

Tips for Strong Comedy Scenes

- Start scenes late and end early. Don't explain what we already understand.
- Use reversals—situations that shift unexpectedly for comedic effect.
- Let characters drive the comedy, not just the jokes.
- Give each character a unique rhythm, vocabulary, and reaction style.
- Use status shifts: someone who's confident in scene one should be humbled by scene three.

Your pilot isn't a showcase of your best jokes—it's a showcase of your show's *comedy engine*. Prove that your premise generates funny situations naturally. Show that your characters are primed for conflict, misunderstanding, and (occasional) emotional insight. Lay the groundwork for a world that can grow, evolve, and deliver fresh laughs every week.

So open up that blank script document. Start with your cold open. Let ChatGPT help you sculpt the beats, punch up the lines, and fill in the gaps. Keep your goal in sight: you're not just writing a funny episode—you're creating the blueprint for a series that could live on screens and in hearts.

Writing Visual Comedy That Doesn't Rely on Dialogue

When we think of comedy, we often think of clever banter, sarcastic quips, and fast-paced dialogue. But some of the funniest moments in television history haven't been spoken—they've been *seen*. A character slowly sliding off a couch while trying to stay cool. Someone hiding under a table while their phone loudly rings. An elaborate physical gag, a perfectly timed look, or an unexpected visual reveal—this is **visual comedy**, and it's an essential tool in your writer's toolkit, especially if you're building a comedy series with staying power.

Visual comedy makes your show feel cinematic. It turns it from a stage play with jokes into a living, breathing experience. And more than that, it travels well. A physical gag is universal. It doesn't need cultural context or subtitles to land. When used well, visual comedy is often what makes a show memorable. Think of *Mr. Bean*, *Fleabag's* lingering eye contact with the camera, *Brooklyn Nine-Nine's* lineup singing "I Want It That Way," or that episode of *Friends* where Ross tries to move the couch—"PIVOT!"—and the scene becomes a slapstick nightmare.

The trick to writing good visual comedy is to stop thinking like a writer and start thinking like a director—or better yet, like an editor. You're not just putting words on a page. You're staging a scene, blocking movement, and planning timing. You're asking, "What will this *look* like?" rather than "What will they say?"

So let's talk technique. First, great visual comedy often stems from **misunderstanding**. Someone doesn't see what we see. The audience knows something the character doesn't—or vice versa. It creates dramatic irony and tension, and the payoff is visual. Maybe your character enters a room where they're supposed to impress someone and doesn't realize they've got a giant rip in the back of their pants. That's not something anyone says. It's something the camera reveals, and the audience sees first. The joke comes from anticipation and the inevitable reveal.

Then there's **physical comedy**—bodies in motion doing things they shouldn't be doing. This isn't just about falling down. It's about intention and failure. The comedy is in the *trying*. Think about Lucille Ball trying to keep up on the chocolate factory conveyor belt. That scene is iconic because of her facial expressions, her panic, and her refusal to give up. You don't need a single line of dialogue to find it hilarious.

Ask ChatGPT for ideas like:

"Give me five visual comedy scenes involving two coworkers trying to install office furniture without reading the instructions."

Or

"What's a wordless gag involving a babysitter, a toddler, and a parrot with attitude?"

Another great visual comedy device is the **reveal**. Hide something in plain sight, then let the audience discover it at just the right moment. A good reveal builds suspense visually. Maybe there's a character acting very calm and collected during a fancy dinner party. The camera pulls back, and we see their pants are on fire. Or they've been hiding a live raccoon in their handbag. The laugh doesn't come from dialogue—it comes from the *difference between what we expected and what we see.*

Use **repetition and escalation** as well. If a visual gag works once, try it again—slightly bigger, slightly dumber, slightly more dangerous. Someone tries to carry too many boxes? Do it again, but now they're on a bike. Do it again, but now they're wearing stilts and being chased by a goose. These kinds of visual riffs are gold because they build momentum and anticipation. And even if the audience knows it's coming, they still want to see how it'll go wrong.

Facial expressions and **reaction shots** are another pillar of visual humor. A deadpan stare. A slow turn. A raised eyebrow. A character reacting to something just off-screen—those tiny, unspoken moments are often funnier than the joke itself. Think about Jim Halpert's glances to the camera in *The Office*. The joke isn't always what Dwight does—it's how Jim *reacts* without saying a word.

When writing your script, describe these moments visually. Don't just say "She's embarrassed." Write:

"Her eyes widen. She freezes. Then, slowly, she sinks behind the couch like a melting snowman."

The more specific you are with the visual behavior, the more clearly the actor and director can see the joke—and the funnier it becomes.

Want to practice? Use ChatGPT to write scenes with zero dialogue. Try:

"Write a 1-minute silent scene where a man tries to sneak into his apartment without waking his dogs, but fails."

You'll start to notice how much storytelling can happen with movement, setting, timing, and visual rhythm alone.

Also remember: **sound design, props**, and **editing** all play into visual comedy, even on the page. A character furiously types on a broken keyboard. Someone sits on what they think is a chair but is actually a cake. The "beat" between a stare and a slap becomes the timing that makes or breaks the gag. You can write all of that into your script—briefly, vividly, and always with an eye on the camera.

One of the best things about using ChatGPT is that you can test visual gags by asking it to simulate different outcomes. You can say:

"What are three increasingly ridiculous visual outcomes of a character trying to open a champagne bottle in a moving car?"

Or

"Write a gag scene where someone tries to hide a dozen cats from a landlord doing a surprise inspection—without speaking."

Visual comedy stretches your creativity beyond words. It challenges you to think about space, silence, contrast, and momentum. It reminds you that some of the most memorable laughs come from what you *show*, not what you say. So when you write your pilot—or any episode—don't rely only on clever dialogue. Ask yourself: how can I make this scene funny even with the sound off?

Your audience—and your future directors—will thank you for it.

Punching Up the Page: One-Liners, Callbacks, and Wordplay

Now that your comedy script is up and running—with structure, character, and story in place—it's time to make it *sparkle*. This is where you add polish, punch, rhythm, and bounce. It's where a solid scene becomes hilarious, where a good character becomes instantly quotable, and where your writing starts to feel like something people will actually *want* to quote back at each other. You've got your story down. Now it's time to punch up the page.

"Punching up" is what writers do in rewrites when they take a decent draft and sharpen the humor. It's adding zing to your zingers. It's trimming fat, twisting phrasing, layering callbacks, and slipping in double meanings. If your story is the engine of your comedy, then the punch-up is the turbo boost—it's what gives your voice that kinetic, unforgettable energy.

Let's start with the most classic tool in the comedy writer's box: **the one-liner**.

A great one-liner isn't just a random joke—it's a character-revealing missile. It says something about the speaker's worldview, their insecurities, their ego, or their sarcasm. Think Chandler in *Friends*. Think Moira in *Schitt's Creek*. Think Rosa in *Brooklyn Nine-Nine*. Their lines are funny because they're *precisely them*. So when you're writing one-liners, don't go for "funny in general." Go for "funny only this character would say."

Ask ChatGPT:

"Write ten one-liners for a character who's emotionally dead inside but very concerned about brunch reservations."

Or:

"Give me punchy insults a know-it-all teen might use without swearing."

A well-placed one-liner can end a scene on a laugh, punctuate a long rant, or completely shift the tone. It can come after a big reveal, a tiny disaster, or even dead silence. You can use them sparingly for impact—or load your dialogue with them if your tone is fast and snappy. Just make sure they flow from the character's voice. A joke is only as good as its context.

Now let's talk about **callbacks**—those beautiful, circular little gifts that reward the audience for paying attention. A callback is when something mentioned earlier returns in a new form, often as a punchline. It creates rhythm, structure, and a sense of control over chaos. A throwaway line in scene one becomes a big laugh in scene five. A minor embarrassment comes back to haunt someone just when they think they've won.

You don't need to plan all your callbacks in advance. You can create them in revision. Read through your script and look for jokes, phrases, or situations that could come back later. Maybe someone brags that they "never cry," and we end the episode with them sobbing over a broken toaster. Maybe a character casually mentions a pet duck and, at the climax, the duck saves the day. The key is surprise with payoff. It feels smart. It feels earned. And it makes the audience feel in on the joke.

To brainstorm callbacks, ask ChatGPT:

"What are three ways I could bring back an earlier joke about a character's fear of escalators for the final scene of the episode?"

Or:

"Suggest a plot twist that turns an earlier insult into the key to saving the day."

Next up: **wordplay**. This includes puns, malapropisms, misheard phrases, double entendres, and literal interpretations of metaphors. It's a staple of clever comedy and works best when it's character-driven. A neurotic character might over-explain a joke. A confident idiot might misuse a word so badly it becomes legendary. Wordplay doesn't have to be highbrow—*Arrested Development* turned bad puns and names into an art form.

Use wordplay to define how characters speak. Maybe one of them constantly misquotes common sayings. Maybe another refuses to use contractions, even when panicking. This kind of linguistic quirk adds texture, rhythm, and memorability to your dialogue. You can also use it to layer in jokes that aren't obvious the first time through but hit hard on rewatch.

Ask ChatGPT:

"Give me examples of malapropisms a character might say instead of common phrases,"

or

"Write a list of wordplay-based insults for a passive-aggressive coworker."

The key to all this is **editing with intention**. Don't write a joke just to fill space—write a joke because it fits the moment, the character, and the tone. You don't need to be funny all the time. In fact, if every line is trying too hard to be clever, the audience will tune out. A good punch-up balances hard laughs with soft chuckles, with silence, with truth. Let the funny lines breathe. Let the visual comedy carry weight when needed. Let characters sit in awkwardness. Comedy is rhythm, not noise.

Here's how to punch up effectively:

1. **Read your script aloud**—or have ChatGPT simulate a table read. You'll hear what drags, what pops, and what lands awkwardly.
2. **Focus on the ends of scenes and lines**. Comedy sticks best at the end of a beat. Trim anything that gets in the way of the punch.
3. **Replace general jokes with specific ones**. "This tastes bad" becomes "This tastes like if regret were a soup."
4. **Make passive lines active**. "That was weird" is fine. "That was like watching two squirrels negotiate a car lease" is better.
5. **Use ChatGPT to heighten a scene**. Ask, "Make this scene 20% funnier while keeping the emotional beat intact."

Remember: your first draft gets the bones in place. Punching up is where you get to *play*. It's where the script becomes alive, where the jokes snap into place, where your show's voice truly comes through. You'll be shocked how much difference one great line can make in a scene.

So grab your script, open your dialogue, and start swinging. The page is yours—and it's time to punch it up.

Designing a Protagonist That Audiences Will Root For and Laugh With

In a comedy series, your protagonist doesn't have to be perfect, polished, or even particularly successful—but they do have to be someone your audience can stick with. They have to be funny, yes, but also deeply human. You want a character that people can laugh at *and* root for. A protagonist who gets into messes, causes their own problems, sabotages their progress, and yet somehow still earns our loyalty. Designing that kind of character is where great comedy begins, and it's a mix of contradictions, quirks, emotional depth, and comic timing.

A strong comedic protagonist is a walking contradiction. They want one thing but do everything in their power to avoid it. They crave connection but push people away. They see themselves as the hero but behave like the problem. That's the sweet spot. These contradictions fuel both plot and humor. Think about Michael Scott from *The Office*: he wants to be loved and respected, but his complete lack of social awareness undermines him at every turn. He's cringe-worthy—but we still root for him because there's vulnerability behind the delusion.

So where do you start?

Start with the **want**. What does your protagonist *want* more than anything else? It should be simple, relatable, and emotionally grounded. They might want approval, fame, love, money, peace, a second chance. It's this core desire that gives the character focus and gives the story momentum. Use ChatGPT to generate possibilities:

"Give me ten funny character motivations for someone trying to escape their family business of psychic frauds."

Then look at the **flaw**. This is what makes the character funny—and human. It could be arrogance, laziness, anxiety, vanity, naivety, obsession, or the inability to read the room. Their flaw is the comic lens through which they approach the world—and it's what gets them into trouble. Think of it as their comedic compass: every time they try to solve a problem, their flaw tilts the needle in the wrong direction.

Ask ChatGPT:

"What are some funny flaws for a character who runs a motivational seminar but secretly hates people?"

Now develop the **voice**. A great comedic protagonist has a distinct way of talking, thinking, and reacting. They don't just deliver jokes—they *are* the joke sometimes, through their phrasing, their timing, their emotional overreactions or underreactions. Think of Fleabag's dry self-commentary, or Leslie Knope's turbo-charged enthusiasm. You can feed a character description into ChatGPT and say:

"Write five lines of dialogue for a character who's painfully polite but slowly unraveling."

You'll start to find a tone and rhythm that fits.

Next, build the **relationship dynamics**. Comedy thrives on contrast, and the protagonist's relationships are often where the funniest moments happen. Who challenges them? Who enables them? Who do they try to impress? Surrounding your protagonist with characters who poke their weaknesses or amplify their delusions keeps the comedy alive and the emotional arcs grounded. Think about who your character needs—and who they *can't stand*—to push them into funny situations.

Ask ChatGPT to help map this out:

"Suggest three character dynamics that would put pressure on a perfectionist teacher in a chaotic school setting."

Let's not forget **vulnerability**. This is what makes your protagonist more than just a joke machine. It's what allows the audience to invest. They may be a mess, but they're *trying*. They care about something, even if they can't say it. Vulnerability gives the comedy context. When the character falls apart, we feel for them even as we laugh. When they succeed—however awkwardly—we cheer.

The protagonist also needs **agency**. They need to drive the story. They shouldn't just react to the world—they should *push* against it. Their bad ideas, poor decisions, and hopeful delusions are what kick-start the chaos. Don't make them passive. Even if they're lazy or avoidant, they should actively avoid things. The funniest protagonists are engines of their own undoing—and they double down even as it blows up in their face.

And finally, give your protagonist **room to grow—or refuse to grow**. Some characters learn. Some never change. Both can work, as long as you're consistent and intentional. A show like *Schitt's Creek* builds its comedy around emotional growth. A show like *Always Sunny in Philadelphia* builds its comedy around emotional stasis. Either way, the character's journey (or lack thereof) gives your series shape.

To bring it all together, try prompting ChatGPT with:

"Design a protagonist for a workplace comedy about a cryogenics facility, including their backstory, flaw, motivation, and personality quirks."

Once you have your protagonist built, test them. Write a few sample scenes. Drop them into ridiculous situations. See how they react when they're embarrassed, when they win, when they're stuck with someone they hate. The more you throw at them, the more their voice will sharpen. Let ChatGPT help by writing scenes like:

"Write a short scene where this character accidentally ruins a retirement party and tries to fix it by making a motivational speech."

Your goal is to create someone who is flawed but not cruel, funny but not a caricature, absurd but emotionally grounded. Someone we can laugh *at* and *with*—sometimes in the same breath.

When you get it right, your protagonist becomes the heart of the show. The one we want to follow through every misadventure, meltdown, and miracle.

And now that your protagonist is ready, let's build the cast around them.

Giving Your Supporting Cast Real Comedy Muscle

If your protagonist is the engine of your comedy series, your supporting cast is the fuel, the spark plugs, the squeaky brakes, and the snacks rolling around in the glove box. They're the friction, the flavor, and the extra laughs that keep the story lively. A weak supporting cast will make your show feel flat and repetitive. A strong one—one that's quirky, dimensional, and well-balanced—can turn a good show into a classic.

The best comedy series are ensemble machines. Even if there's a clear lead, the supporting characters don't just orbit them—they pull their own gravity. Think of Dwight Schrute in *The Office*, Moira Rose in *Schitt's Creek*, Ron Swanson in *Parks and Recreation*, or Rosa Diaz in *Brooklyn Nine-Nine*. These characters have clear personalities, unique rhythms, and comedic potential that's independent from the main storyline. They're not just reacting to the protagonist—they're building their own miniature chaos on the side.

So how do you build a supporting cast with real comedy muscle?

Start with **contrast**. Every strong ensemble is built around differences—of status, personality, communication style, values, energy levels. Contrast creates tension, and tension creates comedy. If your main character is high-energy and manic, pair them with someone slow, chill, and emotionally unreadable. If they're sarcastic, surround them with sincerity. If they're desperate for approval, let them bounce off someone who doesn't even notice they exist.

Ask ChatGPT:

"Give me five character types that would clash in funny ways with a smug, self-help guru protagonist."

Or

"Design a trio of co-workers with wildly different approaches to solving workplace problems."

Then dig into **function**. Each supporting character should serve a purpose in the story. Not in a mechanical, "they move the plot" way—but in how they challenge, expose, or balance out the protagonist. There's the confidant. The rival. The voice of reason. The wildcard. The obstacle. The cheerleader. The chaos agent. The beauty of comedy is that one character can often fill more than one role—and then reverse those roles for fun.

Also ask: **What's funny about this character when they're alone?** If you took the protagonist out of the scene, could this person still carry it? That's a great litmus test. Think of George Costanza in *Seinfeld*. He's got his own flaws, neuroses, and schemes. He doesn't just comment on Jerry—he builds his own mess. You want characters who can exist outside the gravitational pull of your lead.

A strong supporting character also has a **clear voice**. That means not only what they say, but how they say it. Their vocabulary, their rhythm, their tone. Do they rant? Whisper? Misuse big words? Are they hilariously blunt or so indirect that nobody knows what they're talking about? Use ChatGPT to explore this by asking:

"Write three lines of dialogue for a supporting character who's painfully polite but secretly furious."

Or:

"Give me a running gag for a side character who always misquotes inspirational posters."

Now let's talk about **status dynamics**. Comedy often emerges from shifts in power—who's up, who's down, and how that keeps flipping. Your supporting cast should create opportunities for your protagonist to gain or lose status in each episode. Maybe the low-status janitor has the best ideas. Maybe the emotionally fragile intern turns out to be a social manipulator. These reversals create satisfying, surprising moments that deepen the comedy.

You can also build out **pairings** within your supporting cast. Side characters should have chemistry with each other, not just the lead. These relationships give you new combinations to explore: unlikely friendships, silent rivalries, co-conspirators, or total mismatches. Some of the best comedy episodes come from throwing two secondary characters into a plotline and watching them unravel.

A great supporting character also has at least one **weird hill to die on**—a specific belief or obsession that's out of proportion to the world around them. It could be a belief that squirrels are government spies. Or that microwaves erase memory. Or that birthday parties are psychological warfare. These exaggerated viewpoints make for instant jokes and give your characters an angle. They don't need to be quirky for quirk's sake—but a specific worldview is gold.

To brainstorm those quirks, prompt ChatGPT with:

"Give me five oddly specific character traits that could drive long-term running jokes in a comedy series."

Or

"Create a backstory for a supporting character who refuses to use electricity but works in a tech startup."

Don't forget: **emotion still matters.** Even the weirdest characters need a pulse. Give them insecurities, hopes, blind spots, and attachments. Maybe the sarcastic best friend is hiding burnout. Maybe the annoying neighbor is mourning a broken friendship. These human touches make the comedy hit harder, because the audience starts to care. They may laugh at your characters—but they'll also root for them.

And give your supporting cast **room to evolve**. Don't lock them into one note. Let them grow, regress, surprise, and change alliances. Maybe the sidekick becomes the saboteur. Maybe the loner joins a team. Maybe the "funny one" becomes the emotional anchor for a single, unexpected episode. ChatGPT can help outline mini-arcs:

"Describe a three-episode character arc for a background character who suddenly gets promoted and can't handle the power."

When you write scenes, keep an eye on your supporting cast's potential. Who's stealing focus? Who could handle a subplot? Who could carry an episode? These are signs that you're building a comedy world that can last.

So now, open your series bible and flesh out those character bios. Write them like they matter—because they do. They're the friction, the fuel, and often, the fan favourites. The ones whose faces on a T-shirt might sell better than your protagonist's.

Creating Antagonists in a Comedy World

In a traditional drama, the antagonist is the threat, the obstacle, the force the protagonist must overcome. They're powerful, often dangerous, and usually dead serious. But in a comedy? The antagonist can be just as central—only they're not always evil, and they're rarely smooth. In fact, comedy antagonists are often hilarious in their own right. They're stubborn, delusional, weirdly passionate, or simply the wrong person in the wrong place at the wrong time. What makes them effective isn't their menace—it's their *inflexibility*.

Comedy antagonists aren't villains. They're blockers. Disruptors. Contradictions to the protagonist's goals, lifestyle, or worldview. And when they're written right, they become some of the funniest, most iconic characters in the show. Think of Newman in *Seinfeld*, Lucille Bluth in *Arrested Development*, or Captain Holt's endless parade of rivals in *Brooklyn Nine-Nine*. They're the grit in the gears—and we love them for it.

So how do you build a comedy antagonist who truly works?

Start with **what they oppose**. They exist to challenge your protagonist, so ask: what belief, behavior, or plan does your main character have that this person fundamentally disagrees with or threatens? The best antagonists expose flaws in your hero, force them to adapt, and push them into funny situations. Maybe they're an ex who's always one step ahead. Maybe they're a boss who runs the office like a cult. Maybe they're a well-meaning relative who's determined to "fix" your protagonist's life.

Use ChatGPT to help by prompting:

"Give me five comedic antagonist ideas for a protagonist who's trying to start an honest business in a town full of hustlers."

Or

"Design a funny rival character for a people-pleasing kindergarten teacher."

Next, consider **tone**. In comedy, the antagonist doesn't have to be dangerous—they can be wildly over-the-top, painfully sincere, socially oblivious, or bureaucratically terrifying. They can be passive-aggressive or extremely loud. But they *must* be consistent. Their strength comes from how stubbornly they stick to their worldview, even when it makes no sense. Their role is to throw the protagonist off course, not necessarily through violence or betrayal, but through inconvenience, contradiction, or emotional sabotage.

A strong comedy antagonist often works because they believe *they're right*. They might be petty, obsessive, insecure, or overly righteous—but they're always convinced they're doing the right thing. That's where the comedy comes in: watching someone make things worse while thinking they're saving the day. A classic example? Ron Swanson and Tammy 2. They think they're meant for each other... and they destroy everything in their path.

Use ChatGPT to deepen your antagonist with a prompt like:

"Create a comedic antagonist who truly believes they're a hero, even though they're making life miserable for the lead character."

Now think about **status**. Comedy thrives on status shifts—so you'll get a lot of mileage from an antagonist who either *outranks* your protagonist (the boss who never listens) or is *way beneath them* in status but keeps gaining the upper hand.

A low-status antagonist who always wins is inherently funny. Think of Jerry vs. Newman. Newman loses a lot—but every win feels like a personal apocalypse for Jerry.

Comedy antagonists can also be **recurring**, appearing just often enough to stir the pot. They don't need to dominate every episode. They can hover in the background, pop up when least expected, or be part of a running gag. Maybe they're not even a person. Maybe it's a dog, a neighbor's drone, or a sentient toaster. Antagonism doesn't have to be evil—it just has to be persistent.

Try asking ChatGPT:

"What's an unusual recurring antagonist for a character who lives off the grid in a tech-dominated city?"

Or

"Give me a list of five comedic antagonists that could appear once per season and shake up the entire cast."

The best comedic antagonists also bring out **new sides of your protagonist**. They force them to react in unexpected ways. Maybe your charming, chill lead becomes a raging lunatic in the presence of their ex-roommate. Or your quiet introvert starts plotting elaborate revenge schemes when the HOA president fines them for painting their door the wrong shade of red. The antagonist makes the protagonist funnier by pulling them out of their comfort zone.

And don't be afraid to let your antagonists **win sometimes**. Or at least seem like they have. A great comic villain is never truly defeated—they just slink away until next time. Their victories create tension and momentum. The audience wants to see the rematch, the revenge, the next escalation. That's how running gags and long-term rivalries are born.

You can also **humanize** your antagonist without softening their edge. Maybe they're fighting the protagonist because they're heartbroken. Or because they're trying to impress someone. Or because they genuinely think their nemesis is a threat to the greater good. These layers make the comedy deeper—and give you room to surprise the audience when the antagonist suddenly does something noble or shockingly self-aware.

Finally, remember this: in the best comedies, antagonists eventually become part of the family. Maybe they join the group. Maybe they form an uneasy alliance. Maybe they even help save the day—reluctantly, awkwardly, and with a ton of conditions. That's a beautiful arc in itself: from enemy to frenemy to partner-in-chaos. So give your antagonist teeth, give them quirks, give them a mission—and then let them gleefully stand in your protagonist's way, again and again.

How Flawed Should Your Characters Be?

In comedy, perfection is boring. It's the cracks, contradictions, and deeply weird personal hang-ups that make characters funny, lovable, and endlessly watchable. The question isn't whether your characters should be flawed—it's *how flawed is too flawed?* When are they hilarious, and when are they just plain awful? How do you make people laugh at your character's worst moments without losing them altogether? The answer lies in understanding the delicate balance between flaw and empathy, chaos and control, disaster and redemption.

The truth is: **flaws are the fuel of comedy.** They drive conflict, generate tension, and make characters feel real. A character who always says the right thing, acts responsibly, and sees the world clearly is a character who belongs in a PSA, not a comedy. But flaws alone aren't enough. You need to know what kind of flaws create funny, repeatable behavior without turning your characters into cartoon villains or exhausting jerks.

Let's look at a few core categories of comedy flaws and how they work:

There's the **ego flaw**—arrogance, narcissism, delusion. Think of David Brent in *The Office* or Dennis Reynolds in *It's Always Sunny in Philadelphia*. These characters are often completely unaware of how they're perceived, and their delusion drives some of their funniest moments. But the key is that their flaws *reveal them*, not define them entirely. They can still show glimpses of insecurity, vulnerability, or humanity—even if they cover it up with bravado.

Then there's the **emotional flaw**—characters who are anxious, insecure, needy, or oversensitive. These traits make characters highly reactive, which is great for comedy. George Costanza is a master class in this. His flaws are wrapped around his nerves, and his overreactions become the comedy. You don't need your character to be emotionally mature—you just need them to try and fail in funny, recognizable ways.

Some characters lean on **moral flaws**—they lie, cheat, manipulate, or steal. But to make that funny (and palatable), you either need to *outscale* the consequences (*Veep*, *Arrested Development*) or *undermine their success* (*Always Sunny*, *Curb Your Enthusiasm*). These are characters who behave badly but rarely get away with it. Their downfall is built into the joke. And they're usually surrounded by characters who call them out, challenge them, or just roll their eyes at their latest scheme.

Ask ChatGPT to explore these angles:

"Write a scene where a morally questionable character tries to justify stealing a dog because they believe the dog 'chose them instead.'"

Or:

"Create three comedic character flaws that could drive stories without making the character unlikable."

Now consider how far you can go. The golden rule? **You can make characters do terrible things—as long as they suffer for it, learn nothing, or react in a completely unexpected way.** Comedy is about tension without destruction. When someone slips on a banana peel, it's funny because it's harmless chaos. If your character robs a blind man and walks away smiling, that's not flawed—it's just dark. Unless the blind man turns out to be a con artist, and now we're in comedy again.

To guide you, ask: *Is the character's flaw funny because it's universal? Exaggerated? Desperate?* The best comedy flaws are often rooted in truths we recognize but rarely admit. That's why we laugh. A fear of being irrelevant, a need for control, an inability to let go—these are real. When blown up and placed in funny situations, they become comedy gold.

Another trick? **Give your characters blind spots.** Maybe they think they're brave but flee at every loud noise. Maybe they think they're charming but offend everyone in the room. These self-perceptions clash with how the world actually sees them—and those gaps are pure comedy. Use ChatGPT to build on these with prompts like:

"What are three funny contradictions for a character who sees themselves as a wise old soul but lives like an unwashed goblin?"

Also: **scale your flaws to your tone**. In a lighthearted sitcom, your flaws should feel redeemable. In a dark comedy, they can be corrosive. Know your sandbox. *Brooklyn Nine-Nine* allows its characters to be silly and stubborn—but not cruel. *BoJack Horseman* lets its protagonist spiral into self-destruction—but surrounds him with a world that always reflects the consequences back at him.

Most importantly, balance flaws with **a thread of sincerity**. You don't need to make your characters good—you just need to give them *wants*. Even if it's just love, success, or peace and quiet, those desires ground the character and give the audience something to hang onto. The worse their behavior, the more essential that thread becomes. We forgive a lot when we believe someone is trying—even if they fail every time.

Use ChatGPT to generate internal contradictions like:

"Design a character who wants to be respected for their intelligence but keeps pretending to be dumb to avoid responsibility."

So, how flawed should your characters be?

Flawed enough to make trouble.

Flawed enough to drive conflict.

Flawed enough to make the audience laugh, groan, or whisper "same."

But not so flawed that the audience tunes out or stops rooting for them.

They should be a beautiful mess. Like the rest of us.

And now that your characters are flawed in all the right ways, let's explore how to write relationships that make those flaws explode in glorious, funny chaos.

Writing Relationships That Fuel the Laughs

In the world of comedy, a character alone is rarely funny for long. Even the most ridiculous protagonist needs someone to bounce off, challenge them, or just witness their nonsense. That's where relationships come in. More than just background connections, relationships in a comedy series are engines for jokes, tension, reversals, and growth. They're where you get the quick banter, the long burns, the surprising tenderness, and the awkward standoffs. And when you get those dynamics right, the laughs don't come from gags—they come from watching people *collide*.

Comedy thrives on friction, and friction comes from differences. Opposites may attract in romance, but they absolutely *ignite* in comedy. The trick is to design relationships where personalities clash, misunderstandings spiral, and nobody listens as well as they think they do. You want emotional static. You want the well-meaning friend who always makes it worse. The rival who refuses to be outdone. The boss who thinks they're inspirational but inspires only dread. These aren't just character types—they're relationship dynamics, and they power the show.

Start by asking: *what's the emotional gap between these two people?* That gap is your comedy zone. Maybe one is desperate for validation, while the other couldn't care less. Maybe one sees their connection as sacred, while the other forgets their name. Comedy lives in those mismatches. Use ChatGPT to help explore them:

"Give me three odd-couple friendship dynamics for a high-strung overachiever and a blissed-out slacker."

Or

"What's a romantic tension dynamic between two people who are both secretly in love with the same third character?"

One of the best ways to write funny relationships is to **assign roles, then subvert them**. Maybe a character sees themselves as the mentor, the protector, or the leader—but they're none of those things. Maybe the "sidekick" turns out to be the most emotionally stable one in the room. Comedy loves when roles collapse under pressure. Think of Leslie and Ron in *Parks and Recreation*. On the surface, total opposites. In practice, mutual respect laced with bafflement. Their scenes are never boring because they're both so *themselves*.

Another useful angle: **power imbalance**. Comedy relationships often form around who *thinks* they're in charge versus who actually is. A manager and their assistant. A teacher and a gifted student. A parent and their oddly wise kid. Power shifts generate humor, especially when the one with the power keeps losing it. Ask ChatGPT for dynamics like:

"Give me three funny workplace hierarchies where the person at the top is clearly the least competent."

You'll also want to use **emotional stakes**. Not every relationship has to be loud or confrontational. Some of the best comedy comes from repressed affection, weird loyalty, or unresolved history. Maybe they're exes who still live together. Maybe they're best friends from childhood who can't admit they've grown apart. Maybe they're siblings who hate each other—but form a united front when anyone else dares criticize them. These ties give your series depth. They also give you material for callbacks, running gags, and late-season emotional payoffs.

Running gags work beautifully within relationships. Maybe two characters have an ongoing bet that shows up in every episode. Maybe one keeps forgetting the other's birthday. Maybe every time they try to bond, a disaster happens. These patterns become familiar to the audience—and familiar is funny. Use ChatGPT to brainstorm recurring relationship bits:

"What's a funny recurring miscommunication between a character who over-explains and one who's always three steps behind?"

And don't forget to let the **relationships evolve**. Characters who stay stuck aren't funny forever. Maybe the rival becomes an ally. Maybe the love interest becomes the antagonist. Maybe the clueless roommate slowly becomes the voice of reason. Change doesn't have to be dramatic—it just has to be consistent. Let their dynamics shift, even slightly, as they grow (or fail to grow) together. A moment of unexpected honesty can be just as funny as a perfectly timed insult, especially when it catches the other character off guard.

You can also build **ensemble dynamics**. Trios, love triangles, cliques, found families, and work crews give you endless combinations. You don't always need deep character arcs—sometimes you just need two people to be trapped in an elevator with wildly different priorities. The more relational pressure you apply, the funnier the cracks become.

Use ChatGPT to map those combinations:

"List five group dynamics for a comedy ensemble including an optimist, a schemer, a skeptic, and a chaos agent."

Here's a secret: your audience often falls in love with the *relationships*, not just the individuals. They'll quote the banter. They'll ship the couples. They'll root for the weird friendship to survive even when everything goes wrong. So when you build your cast, don't just think about who they are. Think about how they *connect*—and more importantly, how they *don't*. That's where the best laughs live.

Next time you write a scene, ask: *Is this just two people talking? Or is this a dynamic that's getting deeper, funnier, and more complicated with every line?*

If it's the second one, you're doing it right.

The Comic Journey: Where Growth and Gags Intersect

Comedy and growth aren't always the most obvious pair. Growth feels like drama territory—arcs, change, emotional breakthroughs. Comedy, by contrast, seems to be about staying stuck: the character who never learns, never changes, never escapes their loop. But here's the twist. The best comedies don't avoid growth—they just sneak it in. They let characters evolve in small, funny, unexpected ways. They use *gags* to hide the *heart*. That's the comic journey: where the laughs don't just entertain, they reveal the long, awkward, deeply relatable road to becoming a slightly better person.

Or, at least, a different kind of disaster.

Let's be clear—your characters don't have to end the series as completely reformed human beings. They don't need to find happiness, closure, or enlightenment. But the audience still wants to see movement. Even if it's two steps forward, one pratfall back. Even if it's a realization that changes everything—only to be immediately ignored. Comedy has a unique freedom here. It can explore growth without sentimentality. It can let a character try, fail, and keep trying, all while delivering laughs.

So how do you chart the comic journey?

Start by defining your protagonist's **internal contradiction**. What do they want versus what they do to get it? That tension is your through-line. Maybe they want love but push people away. Maybe they want to be respected but lie constantly. Maybe they want peace but keep creating chaos. This is where the jokes and the growth overlap—because their misguided efforts create both the humor and the arc.

Ask ChatGPT for help with a prompt like:

"Design a character who wants stability but keeps impulsively quitting jobs. Describe their comic journey over a season."

Now think in **small shifts**. Comic growth isn't about a single big change—it's about *glimpses* of change. A moment of insight. A rare apology. A surprising act of kindness. These tiny beats feel real because they're earned. And they're funnier when surrounded by characters or events that immediately challenge or derail that progress. Think of Jake Peralta in *Brooklyn Nine-Nine*—immature and reckless, but slowly, over seasons, he becomes a better cop, a more reliable partner, and a decent husband. And he never stops being funny.

Comedy allows for **repetition with evolution**. A character can make the same mistake over and over—but how they *react* to that mistake can shift. Maybe they're less surprised. Maybe they start seeing a pattern. Maybe they even *almost* avoid it—before slipping up again. That's growth in disguise. It's movement inside a loop. It's what keeps your series from becoming a collection of disconnected gags.

Use ChatGPT to brainstorm this with:

"What's a recurring gag that could slowly evolve over a season into a moment of emotional growth?"

Or:

"How might a character's obsession with winning trivia night start as a joke but lead to a serious self-discovery?"

Another tool for the comic journey: **relationships as mirrors**. Your supporting characters should reflect back your protagonist's flaws—and occasionally call them out. A rival who succeeds where they fail. A friend who forgives what they wouldn't. These dynamics show growth not through monologues, but through contrast. Watching someone else change (or refuse to) can kickstart your lead's journey—or highlight how far they still have to go.

It's also smart to let growth come from **failure**, not success. A character doesn't need to get the job, win the date, or fix the mess. Sometimes the loss teaches them something. Sometimes the humiliation is the turning point. Comedy makes failure safe—it turns the worst-case scenario into a laugh. So use it. Break your characters just enough that they have to rebuild something. Even if it's just a better lie.

And don't be afraid to **fake growth** for a joke. Comedy loves false epiphanies. The character who says, "You know what? I learned something today..." only to immediately prove they've learned nothing. That's not wasted space—that's character *definition*. But do it intentionally. If your whole show is built on static characters, that's fine—but make sure the joke is that they *refuse* to grow, not that you forgot to give them a path.

If you want a little more depth, use **season arcs** to track change. You don't need huge shifts every episode, but you can plant milestones: the first time they say no, the first time they open up, the first time they do something for someone else. These moments give your show weight, especially when they're undercut by something hilarious. Growth doesn't need to be clean. It just needs to feel *real.*

Ask ChatGPT to help build those arcs:

"Create a season-long emotional journey for a character who wants to prove they're not a joke—but keeps acting like one."

Or:

"Outline a six-episode arc where a character tries to grow more confident but takes all the wrong advice."

What makes the comic journey unique is that it mirrors *our* lives. We don't change in grand speeches. We change in slow, awkward, clumsy steps. Through embarrassing realizations, arguments with people we care about, and moments of clarity we mostly ignore. That's why growth in comedy feels so powerful—because it sneaks up on you between the jokes. One minute you're laughing at someone getting locked in a closet; the next, you're realizing *they're locked in a pattern they desperately want to break.*

And that's the sweet spot. That's where the gags and growth meet.

So when you're writing your next episode, don't just ask, "What's the joke here?" Ask, "What does this character *almost* learn?" The laugh might land first—but the heart will stick around.

Comedy from Conflict: When Characters Want Opposite Things

Conflict is the backbone of all good storytelling—but in comedy, it's not about swords and showdowns. It's about misunderstandings, mismatched goals, and people talking over each other while pursuing wildly different outcomes. When characters want opposite things, comedy doesn't just emerge—it erupts. It creates tension, awkwardness, desperation, and absurd logic spirals. In other words, it creates exactly the kind of moments that make a comedy series unforgettable.

In this chapter, we're going to look at how to design conflict that's not dramatic in the traditional sense, but *hilariously human*. It's about characters who are each completely justified in their point of view—but completely incompatible in practice. And when their desires collide, the sparks fly.

Let's start with the foundation: **opposing objectives**. One character wants peace and quiet. The other wants to start a one-person brass band. One wants to tell the truth. The other wants to cover up a lie. One wants to break up. The other wants to propose. These oppositions are naturally funny because the collision is inevitable—and that tension builds the joke. The audience knows something's going to break. The only question is *how*.

Use ChatGPT to brainstorm setups like:

"Give me five scene ideas where two characters want completely opposite things in the same moment."

Or:

"Describe a comedic situation where a character wants a serious conversation and the other thinks it's a game."

In comedy, conflict doesn't have to be *loud*—it just has to be *persistent*. Sometimes it's emotional. One person wants intimacy, the other wants distance. Sometimes it's logistical. One wants to host a party, the other already promised to housesit in silence. Sometimes it's philosophical. One believes in karma, the other in chaos. The comedy comes from how these opposing forces keep getting tangled in each other.

Great sitcoms build entire episodes around these kinds of clashes. In *Friends*, Rachel wants to get closure—Ross wants to avoid the conversation. In *Schitt's Creek*, Johnny wants to run the motel like a professional—Roland wants to keep things "casual." The tension is character-based, not plot-driven. You're not forcing conflict; you're letting it grow from who these people are.

To build strong comic conflict, define *what each character believes they need*. Not just on the surface, but emotionally. Maybe a character "just wants to win the bake sale," but what they *really* want is to feel respected. Another "just wants the day off," but what they *really* want is to avoid being seen as a failure. When these deeper wants bump up against each other, the scenes become funnier, faster, and more layered.

Ask ChatGPT:

"Create a character conflict where two people are fighting over a shared workspace, but it's really about identity and self-worth."

The secret is that neither character has to be the villain. In fact, the best comedy conflicts happen when both sides are *right*—or at least think they are. The comedy isn't in who wins; it's in how far they'll go to get what they want, and how wildly off-course things get as a result. That's when you get snowball scenes, misunderstanding montages, and brilliantly avoidable disasters.

Another way to amp up comedy conflict is through **power dynamics**. Who has authority—and how do they misuse it? A character might be "in charge" but emotionally unstable. Another might be "low-status" but somehow always gets their way. Shifting that balance during the conflict creates rhythm. Maybe one starts with the upper hand, but by the end, they're the one tied to a chair by their own shoelaces. These reversals are fun because they reflect the instability of real power—especially in workplace or family comedies.

You can also use **shared goals with incompatible methods**. Two characters want the same thing, but they completely disagree on how to get it. They both want to impress the boss—but one plans a slick pitch, and the other shows up with a singing telegram. They both want to protect a secret—but one chooses silence while the other fabricates a bizarre story involving ninjas and narcolepsy. These setups allow for cooperation *and* chaos.

Prompt ChatGPT for moments like:

"Create a scene where two characters both want to save their friendship but approach it in opposite, funny ways."

Conflict can also be built around **stakes that are absurdly mismatched**. One character is trying to win a legal battle. The other is trying to finish a sandwich. The more serious one character is, the funnier it is when the other completely fails to meet them there. This imbalance in urgency is pure comedy. The character who's underreacting becomes the wild card. The one overreacting becomes the engine.

And don't forget about **conflict as escalation**. A small disagreement can spiral into chaos through miscommunication, pride, or refusal to let go. Maybe someone borrows a mug. Suddenly, there's a full-blown office cold war, secret alliances, and a fake tribunal. Escalation is about letting characters take things way too far for reasons that feel *justified to them*. It's irrational behavior grounded in sincere emotion.

Ask ChatGPT:

"List three scenarios that could start with a simple argument and escalate into total absurdity within a workplace comedy."

And here's the final key: once you've created the conflict, use **resolution to surprise the audience**. Maybe it fizzles out in a moment of strange vulnerability. Maybe someone wins—but it's clearly a hollow victory. Maybe both characters forget what they were even fighting about. Resolution isn't about tying things up neatly. It's about adding one more twist that deepens the character dynamic, sets up the next clash, or just leaves the audience laughing in disbelief.

So, when you're writing your next episode, don't ask, "What's the problem in this scene?" Ask, "What do these characters *want*, and why can't they both have it?"

Because the moment their needs collide, the comedy begins.

Developing Comedic Archetypes with a Twist

In comedy, archetypes are your best starting point—and your biggest trap. Audiences instantly recognize a type: the know-it-all, the clueless optimist, the bitter realist, the lovable idiot. These characters are familiar, and that's useful because it lets the jokes land quickly. But lean too hard on a stock version of a character and your series starts to feel like a rerun. The key is to use comedic archetypes as blueprints—not boxes. Start with the type, then twist it. That twist is where originality, surprise, and long-term laughs live.

Archetypes work because they come with built-in conflict. The perfectionist and the slob. The charmer and the grump. The overachiever and the slacker. We know how these people operate, and we know exactly how they're going to frustrate each other. But when you give them unexpected layers—flaws that don't fit the stereotype, goals that contradict the surface, or a secret softness—they stop being tropes and start becoming unforgettable characters.

Let's look at a few classic comedic archetypes and how to twist them into something fresh:

The Know-It-All

Normally smug, confident, and annoying—always trying to correct people. Now twist it. What if they know *a lot* but are desperate for approval? What if they're constantly fact-checking themselves mid-sentence? Or maybe they're a know-it-all who only knows useless trivia and can't handle real-life decisions.

Ask ChatGPT:

"Write a character description for a know-it-all who's always *technically* right, but still makes everything worse."

The Slacker

This type avoids work, underperforms, and has a can of soda glued to their hand. But what if the slacker has bursts of brilliance and deep emotional intelligence? What if their laziness is strategic—a coping mechanism for anxiety? Or maybe they're only a slacker in certain parts of their life but are wildly over-ambitious in strange, obsessive hobbies.

The Control Freak

The neat freak, the micromanager, the one who schedules bathroom breaks. Normally, this character is rigid and humourless. But what if they secretly love chaos and use their control to create it? What if they're controlling because they grew up in a circus? Give them an unexpected backstory, a blind spot, or a total meltdown waiting to happen.

The Lovable Idiot

Everyone's favorite punchline machine—the doofus who means well but barely functions. To twist this, what if they're only stupid socially but are a brilliant strategist? Or what if they're incredibly insightful but pretend to be dumb because people like them more that way? Or maybe their "idiocy" is more about wild, childlike logic that *occasionally* turns out to be genius.

Use ChatGPT to explore variants:

"List five character quirks that could make a lovable idiot character surprisingly competent in a comedy series."

The Cynic

They've seen it all. Nothing impresses them. Everyone else is an idiot. That's fertile ground for comedy—but also predictability. So twist it: what if they're a cynic who secretly writes romance novels under a pen name? What if they're only cynical because they're terrified of failing at sincerity? Or what if their cynicism is aimed at the world, but they're fiercely loyal to the people they love?

The Optimist

The sunshine character who sees the good in everything—even when it's clearly a disaster. They're delightful, but they can become annoying if not grounded. So give them darkness. Maybe they're an optimist because they're actively *choosing* hope after something awful. Maybe they're using positivity as denial. Or maybe their relentless optimism comes with a weird, unnerving intensity—like they might snap at any moment.

The Chaos Agent

Every show needs one. The wildcard. The person who makes things worse just by existing. But to twist this archetype, what if they actually *do* have a plan? What if their chaos is carefully calibrated? Or what if they desperately want to stop creating chaos but can't seem to help it? That internal contradiction makes them rich and unpredictable.

Now let's talk about combinations. Some of the best comedic characters are **two archetypes at war within the same person**. The narcissist who genuinely wants to do good. The control freak who can't control their own love life. The optimist with anger issues. These contrasts keep your characters surprising, layered, and hard to pin down. And that keeps the audience engaged.

Try a ChatGPT prompt like:

"Design a character who blends the traits of a romantic idealist and a ruthless opportunist in a funny, human way."

Also, let's not forget about **casting archetypes against expectations**. What if the sweet grandma character is secretly running a pyramid scheme? What if the tough-guy security guard has an encyclopaedic knowledge of ballet? When you subvert expectations, you generate comedy just by showing the world the character doesn't match their packaging. Audiences *love* being surprised—and the right twist on an archetype is often enough to carry entire storylines.

As you build your supporting cast, try this exercise: define each character in terms of an archetype, then add at least two traits that *clash* with that type. A nervous seducer. A charming pessimist. A quiet narcissist. The twist shouldn't cancel the archetype—it should *complicate* it. This makes dialogue funnier, relationships richer, and scenes more dynamic.

You can even use ChatGPT to push this process further:

"Give me three ways to twist the 'quirky best friend' trope into a unique comedic character who could steal every scene."

Comedy needs characters who feel big and bold—but also real and surprising. So lean into archetypes. Use them to build your foundation. But then twist them. Break them open. Let the unexpected flaws, fears, and contradictions shine through.

That's how you create characters who aren't just funny for a moment—but funny *forever*.

Next, let's talk about how to design the world that supports these characters—and makes every scene feel alive.

Setting the Scene for Humor: Where Your Series Takes Place

Comedy isn't just what's said or who says it—it's *where* it happens. The setting of your series isn't just background dressing. It's a comedic partner. It creates pressure, limits choices, fuels absurdity, and provides visual contrast for characters and conflict. A great comedy setting helps shape the kind of jokes you can write, the kind of people who belong there, and the kind of chaos they'll inevitably cause. In short, your setting becomes a character itself—one with its own quirks, rhythms, and rules.

Think about the most iconic comedy series and their locations. *The Office* has Dunder Mifflin, a beige, fluorescent hellscape of forced productivity. *Brooklyn Nine-Nine* lives inside a police precinct where professionalism and absurdity collide daily. *Cheers* is literally one bar, but it never runs out of jokes because of who walks in the door. Each setting tells you, even before anyone speaks, what kind of show you're in for. So the question is: where is your comedy truly *at home*?

Start with tone. Is your series grounded and realistic? Then your setting might be mundane but richly specific—a hardware store, a day-care, a dentist's office, a cramped family home. Is your show absurd, surreal, or stylized? Then your setting can be strange or heightened—a cryogenics facility, a post-apocalyptic shopping mall, a cloud-based startup where no one knows what they're selling. The setting sets the *rules* of your comedy world. It tells the audience how weird they should expect things to get.

Ask ChatGPT to help generate ideas:

"List ten unique comedy series settings that haven't been overdone and offer potential for strong character dynamics."

Or

"What's an unusual small-town business that could be the main setting for an ensemble comedy?"

One powerful move is to choose a **constrained environment**. When your characters are trapped—or at least stuck together—it creates constant tension. A failing diner. A support group. A remote Arctic research station. The limitation becomes a comedy pressure cooker. You don't need sprawling geography—you need a tight space where people can't escape each other's flaws. That's what builds friction, and friction is funny.

Another way to think about setting is **how it creates obstacles**. Does your location come with rules your characters hate? People they can't avoid? Situations they can't control? Maybe your show is set in a co-op housing building with endless bureaucracy. Or a church that's trying to modernize under a painfully outdated priest. The setting becomes funny not because of what it is, but because of what it *prevents* the characters from doing.

Great comedy settings also allow for a revolving door of stories. Think of a theme park. A dog grooming salon. A radio station. These spaces invite new characters and scenarios without stretching logic. You can bring in guest characters, one-off stories, or repeat customers that add new chaos to the established dynamic. This kind of setting is generous—it keeps giving you material.

Ask ChatGPT:

"Describe a setting for a comedy series that allows a new 'guest' character every episode while still keeping a strong core ensemble."

Don't forget **visual comedy opportunities**. A great setting should give your characters things to do, touch, bump into, or ruin. If your show takes place in a bakery, there are pies to drop. If it's on a cruise ship, there are endless ways to get lost or overboard. If it's a government office, there are stacks of paperwork that can literally bury someone. Physical space is part of the joke.

Also consider **symbolism**. The setting can reflect your themes. If your show is about failure and false starts, maybe it's set in a doomed start-up hub where every business closes within a month. If it's about reinvention, maybe it's in a community center full of people trying to "start fresh" in the most chaotic ways possible. The setting supports the story beneath the story.

And sometimes, the funniest settings come from placing *the wrong people in the wrong place*. A punk band trying to run a retirement home. A group of conspiracy theorists operating out of a mall kiosk. A hyper-rational scientist teaching kindergarten. It's not just about the place—it's about who absolutely does *not* belong there and what happens when they try to blend in.

To push the boundaries, ask ChatGPT:

"Give me five comedic premises where characters are stuck in a setting they clearly weren't built for."

You also need to think long-term. Can your setting generate stories *season after season*? Does it evolve? Can new characters be introduced logically? Can the location itself become part of a character's arc? In *Schitt's Creek*, the town is a punchline at first—but eventually becomes a place of growth. In *Community*, Greendale is a joke—but also the glue. The best settings don't just hold the comedy—they reflect it back, episode after episode.

Lastly, know your **production limits**—even if it's just imaginary for now. A comedy that's supposed to take place on the International Space Station might be clever on paper, but hard to visualize consistently. (Unless it's animated or has a *very* understanding effects team.) So keep your setting bold but producible. Sometimes the simplest setting—a house, a café, a public pool—becomes iconic because of how creatively you use it.

So what does your comedy series setting *say* before a single line is spoken? Does it challenge your characters? Limit them? Embarrass them? Give them too much power or too little?

If it can do any—or all—of those things, you're in the right place.

Worldbuilding for Laughs—Without Going Overboard

When we think of "worldbuilding," we usually picture fantasy epics or deep sci-fi sagas. Elaborate maps, made-up languages, complex hierarchies, and thousand-page bibles explaining every corner of a fictional universe. But worldbuilding isn't just for dragons and dystopias. In comedy, worldbuilding matters too—and when done right, it makes your jokes sharper, your characters stronger, and your show unforgettable. The key is to build *just enough* world to support the humor—without drowning it in detail.

So, what does worldbuilding mean in a comedy series?

It means defining the rules of your setting—social, emotional, and logical. It means deciding what kinds of absurdity are possible, how far your reality bends, and what kind of people exist in your world. It means creating a place that feels specific enough to generate unique situations, but open enough to allow for surprises.

The first step is figuring out your **comedy logic scale**. Where does your show live on the spectrum between grounded and surreal? A show like *The Office* or *Derry Girls* lives in a heightened but recognizable reality—characters are strange, but the world still operates like the one we know. On the other hand, *30 Rock* or *Rick and Morty* exist in worlds where logic breaks down for the sake of the joke, and reality is flexible if not entirely optional.

Ask ChatGPT:

"Help me define the comedy logic rules for a show set in a retirement home where the staff are all failed magicians."

Or:

"What's the tone difference between a grounded workplace comedy and an absurdist workplace comedy, in terms of worldbuilding?"

Next, identify the **core institutions and customs** that shape your world. In a comedy, this could be the weird internal rules of a failing start-up, the politics of a shared apartment building, or the culture of a deeply dysfunctional town council. These institutions give you recurring characters, catchphrases, running gags, and story engines. They also give your characters something to push against—or desperately cling to.

You don't need to create encyclopaedias. Instead, try this rule of thumb: *build what your characters would notice.* A perfectionist will pay attention to how things are organized (or disorganized). A slacker will care where the snack stash is hidden. A romantic will know who's dating whom, even if they pretend not to care. The world should be filtered through the eyes of your characters—what they value, what they ignore, what they constantly misinterpret.

You can even write micro-rules for your world. For example:

- In this office, nobody knows what the company actually does.
- In this town, there's a local festival every month—each more dangerous than the last.
- In this school, the students are normal, but the faculty have secret soap opera-level backstories.

Use ChatGPT to brainstorm:

"List five weird internal traditions that a small-town city council might enforce in a sitcom setting."

Or:

"What are some world quirks for a comedy series set in a post-apocalyptic chain restaurant?"

A helpful approach is to anchor your worldbuilding in **recurring elements**. Running jokes about the same delivery guy showing up at the worst times. A mysterious locked door in the break room no one mentions. A radio station that constantly announces the wrong weather. These details make the world feel lived-in—and they give you tools to build jokes over time. You're not just writing scenes; you're writing inside a *system*.

The trick is knowing when to stop. Overbuilding your world can create *comedy clutter*. If your audience needs a user's manual to understand the humor, you've gone too far. Comedy works best when the world feels intuitive, even when it's strange. Your job is to introduce rules quickly, use them creatively, and keep the focus on the characters. The world should elevate the humor, not overshadow it.

Try testing your world with this question: *Could you explain the rules of your show in 30 seconds or less?*

If yes, you've built the right amount. If no, strip it back.

And don't forget: worldbuilding is dynamic. You can introduce new quirks as you go—just stay consistent. If you decide that all meetings in your office comedy are required to be conducted via walkie-talkie, great. But now that's part of the world's logic. Build off it. Let characters resist it, exploit it, or forget to follow it with ridiculous results.

Also, worldbuilding is a goldmine for **visual gags and physical comedy**. What's in the background? What's written on the posters in the hallway? What weird rules are posted on the break room bulletin board? These little elements can make your scenes feel funnier without anyone even speaking.

Let ChatGPT help with world details like:

"What's a list of absurd signs you might find in the staff lounge of a comedy set in a cursed amusement park?"

Or:

"Give me ten comedic rules for a fictional apartment complex with an overzealous landlord."

In the end, your comedy world should feel like a playground—built enough to support the jokes, loose enough to surprise you, and specific enough to belong to *your* show and no one else's. Whether it's a single location or an entire town, let it reflect the themes of your series. If your show is about reinvention, maybe the world is full of second-chance businesses and recycled identities. If it's about ambition, maybe everyone's faking their way through a fake-it-'til-you-make-it culture.

Worldbuilding for comedy isn't about creating a perfectly logical universe. It's about crafting a setting where chaos feels natural, rules are meant to be broken, and the world itself sometimes feels like it's laughing *with* you—and sometimes *at* your characters.

And now that your world is in place, let's zoom in even closer—onto the themes that make all of this matter. Funny is good. Funny *with meaning*? Even better.

Themes That Add Depth without Killing the Comedy

Comedy doesn't have to be shallow to be funny. In fact, the funniest, longest-lasting comedies usually aren't just about laughs—they're about *something*. They sneak depth in between the punchlines. They use jokes to explore fear, insecurity, love, identity, or failure. A great comedy can say what dramas can't, because it catches you off guard. You're laughing, and then suddenly—you're hit with a moment that feels weirdly true. That's the magic of theme in comedy. When done right, it adds weight without taking away the bounce.

So how do you build meaningful themes into your comedy series *without* slowing it down, sentimentalizing it, or dragging your show into a full-blown drama?

Start with the simplest rule: **don't tell—*show the contradiction.*** Comedy is all about contradiction. Characters say one thing and do another. They chase happiness in all the wrong places. They deny what they want until it bursts out sideways. This behavior *is* the theme. If your show is about the fear of being forgotten, don't write long speeches about legacy—create a character who throws themselves into every party, every project, every wild distraction just to stay relevant. Then let the jokes grow out of their desperate attempts.

Ask ChatGPT for ideas like:

"Give me three character behaviors that reveal a fear of failure without explicitly stating it."

Or:

"How would a theme of impostor syndrome play out comedically in a workplace sitcom?"

Pick a theme your characters can argue about—or at least reflect differently. If the theme is "everyone wants to be loved," show it through different lenses. One character might seek fame, another clings to a toxic relationship, another hides behind detachment. Their conflicting strategies create friction and misunderstanding, and *that's* your comedy. Theme isn't just an idea—it's a fuel for conflict, dialogue, and absurd behavior.

Themes also help give your comedy **emotional stakes**, even if they're subtle. *BoJack Horseman* deals with depression and self-worth. *Fleabag* tackles grief, guilt, and loneliness. *The Good Place* asks what it means to be a good person. But none of these shows forget to be funny. They just recognize that laughter often *comes from* pain—or our attempts to avoid it. You can make someone cry while they're laughing, or laugh while they're thinking. Both are wins.

Try this exercise: write your theme as a question, not a statement.

Instead of "This show is about friendship," ask: *Can you stay friends with someone you've outgrown?*

Instead of "This show is about identity," ask: *If no one knew who you were, who would you pretend to be?*

The question form keeps the show open, curious, and alive. It invites conflict and contrast. Comedy loves questions with no easy answers.

Use ChatGPT to expand on this with:

"Turn the theme 'fitting in' into a series of questions that could shape character arcs and episode stories."

Or:

"List ten thematic questions that could work for a bittersweet comedy about a struggling artist collective."

Also, make your theme *character-driven*. Don't build the whole world around the theme. Let it emerge from how your characters live, speak, and screw up. If your theme is fear of growing up, don't make everyone talk about maturity—just show your characters refusing to throw away old clothes, failing to commit, obsessing over high school wins, or getting jealous of friends who've moved on. Make the laughs do the talking.

And don't be afraid to **undercut your theme with comedy**. If a character finally has a deep emotional breakthrough, you can immediately follow it with something absurd, ironic, or low-stakes. Think of it as pressure and release. The audience gets to feel something *and* laugh—sometimes at the same time. That balance keeps your show from tipping too far in one direction.

Ask ChatGPT to help you tone-match:

"Write a scene that balances a theme of emotional loneliness with a funny misunderstanding about soup."

Or:

"Suggest five visual gags that echo a theme of never feeling in control."

Themes also help with **season arcs**. They give shape to what your characters are unconsciously working through. If your theme is about self-worth, maybe your protagonist spends the season trying to prove themselves through work, relationships, or image—only to realize their value isn't tied to any of it. Even if every episode is funny and light, the arc adds cohesion. You can call it a "quiet spine"—not something loud or preachy, but something you can feel holding it all together.

Remember: **the theme doesn't need to be serious to be real.** A show can explore ideas like "Is winning actually worth it?" or "What's the cost of always pretending to be okay?" without slowing down. In fact, those ideas can give jokes even more bite. They create tension. They give the comedy a little shadow—and shadow makes the light pop.

Lastly, trust your audience. You don't need to hammer the theme every five minutes. People will feel it. They'll start to see the pattern in how characters behave, how episodes end, and what your protagonist keeps messing up. Theme is what the audience takes home with them after the laughs fade. It's the echo. The tug. The reason your show lingers. So go ahead—pick your theme. Let it simmer under the scenes. Let it shape your characters without defining them. Let it turn a funny moment into one that matters. Because the best comedy doesn't just make us laugh.

It makes us *care*.

Writing Comedy That Feels Fresh Without Trying Too Hard

There's nothing more exhausting than comedy that's desperate to be funny. You can spot it a mile away—the over-punchy dialogue, the forced randomness, the characters who sound like they're competing for Twitter likes instead of living in a story. It's loud, brittle, and oddly joyless. So how do you write comedy that feels *fresh*, surprising, and alive—without trying so hard it starts to sweat?

The answer lies in confidence, clarity, rhythm, and truth. Fresh comedy doesn't come from layering ten punchlines into every line—it comes from knowing your characters, trusting the setup, and letting the humor *breathe*. And most importantly, it comes from writing situations, not just jokes.

Let's start with the core idea: **you don't have to reinvent the wheel**. You just have to spin it in your voice. Almost every story in comedy is a remix—two people stuck together, a lie that spirals, someone wanting something they can't get. It's how you *twist* it that makes it feel new. The unexpected detail. The left-field reaction. The truth behind the absurdity.

So if your setup feels familiar—great. That's actually a strength. Just make sure the specifics are *yours*. A character trying to hide a secret date isn't new. But if it's happening in the middle of a silent meditation retreat, or while they're also pretending to be allergic to romance for social clout—that's new. Ask ChatGPT for help with this:

"Give me five fresh angles on a classic sitcom setup: two people try to plan a surprise party for the same person and don't know it."

Or

"What are some new spins on the 'roommate rules' conflict for a comedy pilot?"

Another way to keep things fresh is by focusing on **authentic reactions**. A tired comedy beat is when everyone in a scene sounds like they're in the same writer's room. Instead, write characters who don't understand each other. Characters who derail each other. Characters who are in two different emotional gears at the same time. One's trying to open up emotionally; the other's obsessed with figuring out who stole their yogurt. That disconnect *is* the comedy.

Freshness also comes from **restraint**. You don't have to hammer a joke for it to land. You don't even need to call attention to it. The best comedies trust the audience. They let a glance, a pause, or a bad idea hang in the air. They don't explain the punchline. They don't add a second joke to top the first. They know when to stop. Use ChatGPT to test this:

"Rewrite this scene to make it feel 20% funnier just by adjusting rhythm, pauses, and understatement—no new jokes."

Tone discipline helps too. A show that throws in sarcasm, sentimentality, fourth-wall breaks, slapstick, and nihilism all in the same scene might *technically* be unpredictable—but it's exhausting. Pick your tone and let it guide the comedy. If your show's grounded, let the jokes come from awkwardness, honesty, or quiet reversals. If it's heightened, go big—but keep it consistent. The goal is rhythm, not randomness.

And speaking of randomness—**weird isn't automatically fresh**. Just because something is bizarre or unexpected doesn't mean it's funny. A giant squirrel showing up in the middle of a scene might be surprising, but without context, tone, or setup, it's just noise. Let your weirdness have *rules*. Let it grow out of character or world logic. When the surprise fits the emotional tone, it feels clever. When it's thrown in just to be edgy, it dies.

Another strategy? **Mine the mundane.** Some of the freshest comedy comes from taking something deeply ordinary and exposing the chaos inside it. A car ride. A Zoom call. A birthday card. It's all funny when you zoom in far enough. The trick is specificity. Don't just say "he's nervous about a date"—show him trimming nose hairs in his rear-view mirror using an empty CD case. These hyper-specific, grounded, absurd details are gold.

Ask ChatGPT for detail-generation like:

"List five funny and original things a nervous character might do to prepare for a big date without realizing they're making it worse."

And here's a powerful truth: **fresh comedy often comes from point of view.** Your show doesn't need to be the *most* outrageous, or the most subversive. It needs to feel like *your* take. What annoys you? What confuses you? What's something about people that you notice but others don't talk about? That's your lens. When characters speak with a clear, unique perspective—even if the topic is familiar—it feels new.

This is especially useful when using ChatGPT. You can take a prompt like:

"Write a scene about a character trying to quit their job,"

then say:

"Now rewrite it from the POV of someone who thinks quitting is a spiritual experience."

or

"Rewrite it from someone who only speaks in movie quotes but doesn't realize it."

And here's the last key: **write what's *funny to you*—then test and trim.** If you laugh while writing it, great. If you read it the next day and it still holds up, even better. If not—cut it. Comedy is clarity. If a line doesn't move the story forward or reveal character or land the laugh, it's just filler. Don't cling to the clever idea that doesn't serve the moment. That's how comedy becomes clunky and overworked.

Fresh comedy doesn't feel like it's trying to be funny. It feels like it *is* funny—because it's rooted in voice, character, and truth. So take your time. Let your characters surprise you. Let your tone guide you. Let the situation build naturally. Then, when the laugh comes, it'll feel earned.

And the audience? They'll laugh *with* your show—not *at* its effort to be funny.

Humor and Humanity: Finding the Heart behind the Gags

Great comedy isn't just about the joke—it's about the person telling it, why they're telling it, and what they're trying to hide or reveal. The best comedy makes us laugh *and* feel something. It sneaks truth in behind absurdity. It lets us see ourselves in characters who are falling apart, messing up, acting petty, or trying too hard. That's the heart behind the gags. That's what makes your series more than just clever—it makes it human.

Humor is often a defense mechanism. It's how characters deflect pain, avoid connection, or gain control in situations where they feel powerless. That's where you find emotional depth—not by turning your show into a drama, but by recognizing that comedy and vulnerability don't cancel each other out. They enhance each other. They work best when they're in tension. Because when someone cracks a joke while their world is cracking underneath them, we *feel* that. And we laugh because we recognize the truth in it.

To write comedy with heart, you have to start with **what your characters care about**—not what they say they care about, but what they actually *need*. Maybe they need to be loved, respected, seen, forgiven. Now build your jokes around the ways they fail to get those needs met. That's the sweet spot: the intersection of longing and laughter.

Use ChatGPT to explore that with prompts like:

"Describe a character who uses sarcasm to mask loneliness—give me three scenes where this creates humor and heartbreak simultaneously."

Or:

"Write a moment where a character makes a joke at their own expense but clearly wants someone to stop laughing and actually listen."

Next, build your comedy out of **honest behavior**, not just punchlines. When a character acts in a way that's real—even if it's ridiculous—it resonates. Think about how a person who's afraid of being left out might overcompensate. They might lie about being invited somewhere, or throw a party they clearly can't afford. It's funny—but it's also sad. That's where the heart is. You don't have to say it out loud. The audience will *see* it in the choices.

Also, trust **the pauses between the jokes**. Not every line needs a laugh. In fact, the most powerful comedy often comes from the contrast between a funny scene and a sudden moment of sincerity. Maybe two characters are arguing, the fight escalating into absurd territory—and then, one of them admits something real, something small, something vulnerable. Don't overwrite it. Let it land. Let the silence hang before the next laugh resets the rhythm. It makes the emotional moment stick.

Ask ChatGPT to help craft that contrast:

"Write a scene that begins as a physical comedy sequence and ends with a quiet moment of emotional clarity—without losing the humor."

Another way to find heart is to explore **relationships beneath the jokes**. What does one character *really* mean when they tease another? Why does a running gag annoy one person and comfort another? Comedy is packed with subtext—sometimes a joke is just a joke, and sometimes it's a love letter or a cry for help wrapped in laughter. Your job is to make sure that those layers are present, even if they're not spoken aloud.

Characters don't have to be sweet to be human. Some of the most heartfelt comedy comes from deeply flawed, resistant people. People who sabotage themselves. Who push people away. Who are terrified of being seen. The heart comes through when the audience starts to understand *why*. You can make a character say the most awful things—but if we get even a flicker of the wound underneath, we'll keep watching. We'll root for them, even if they don't root for themselves.

Use ChatGPT to deepen flawed characters like this:

"Give me a character profile for someone who always makes fun of others but is secretly afraid no one likes them."

Also, don't shy away from **bittersweet moments**. Not every resolution needs to be happy. Sometimes the comedy builds to a win that's messy, a revelation that doesn't solve anything, or a joke that turns out to be truer than anyone wanted it to be. These moments linger. They give your show texture. Humor without heart is forgettable. Heart without humor can get heavy. But blend them, and you get something people return to, again and again.

One of the smartest moves you can make is to **let characters grow—just a little**. Comedy doesn't have to freeze characters in place. They can stumble toward self-awareness. They can make progress they immediately undo. They can change just enough to keep us curious. This emotional momentum adds purpose to your humor. It doesn't make your show "serious"—it makes it satisfying.

So ask yourself:

What does your protagonist truly want—but won't admit?

What emotion lives just beneath their most-used joke?

What's the one thing they can't laugh about yet?

That's your heart.

And when you find it, don't spotlight it. Don't over-explain. Let it flicker under the gags. Let it show up in the way someone leaves a room, or stays quiet after a joke doesn't land. Let the audience discover it on their own. That's what makes it stick.

In the end, what makes a comedy *great*—not just funny—is its ability to remind us we're all messy, hopeful, scared, absurd, and trying our best. And sometimes the only thing we can do is laugh.

Next, we'll talk about **comedic rhythm**—how to shape scenes that keep the laughter flowing without burning out the audience or the momentum. Because heart matters. But timing is everything.

Pacing Your Comedy So the Laughs Keep Coming

Comedy is rhythm. It's not just about what's funny—it's about *when* it lands. Great jokes fall flat when the pacing is off, and even a mediocre gag can kill if the setup and timing are perfect. Pacing in comedy isn't just about how fast things move. It's about *how well* each moment earns its space. It's the balance between setup and payoff, between silence and noise, between emotional beats and laugh-out-loud chaos.

When you pace your comedy right, it feels effortless. The jokes roll, the energy builds, the surprises pop, and the audience never feels like they're waiting for the next laugh—or being buried under too many. So how do you shape your script so the laughs keep coming without overwhelming the story or the audience?

Start with the **scene-level rhythm**. A typical comedic scene often runs three to four minutes (sometimes shorter), and should accomplish *one thing well*—either build to a punchline, escalate a situation, flip a power dynamic, or reveal something funny about a character. If your scene is just there for exposition or filler, cut it or give it a twist. Comedy scenes shouldn't wander. They should have shape—like a little mini-sketch with a beginning, middle, and payoff.

Use ChatGPT to explore shape like:

"Write a short scene that starts with a misunderstanding, escalates with a lie, and ends with a visual gag."

Or:

"Outline a three-beat structure for a workplace comedy scene about someone trying to hide a birthday surprise."

Now zoom out and look at the **episode rhythm**. You want variety. A breathless run of high-energy scenes will wear out your audience. Likewise, too many low-key, talky moments in a row can lull the viewer into checking their phone. You need waves. Peaks and valleys. A big, chaotic scene followed by a quiet, awkward moment. A long build-up followed by a quick, sharp release. This variety keeps your show *alive*. It gives the audience time to laugh, to reset, to get ready for the next moment.

Think about **joke density**. Not every line needs to be a punchline. You want the laughs to come consistently, but not constantly. Too many jokes and nothing lands. Too few, and you lose momentum. A good rule is to vary the kinds of laughs—mix in hard jokes, soft chuckles, visual gags, physical beats, and character moments. Let a character's body language or a callback earn the laugh instead of always chasing the next zinger.

Use ChatGPT to assess or improve a scene's balance:

"Analyze this scene and suggest ways to adjust the pacing for better comedic rhythm."

Or:

"Rewrite this scene to improve timing—keep the emotional beat but spread out the jokes more strategically."

Also consider the **emotional pacing**. Your show isn't just a joke delivery machine—it's about people. So ask: when do you slow down to let a moment land? When do you push forward to keep the energy up? The best comedies often sneak in sincerity between the chaos. A quick heart-to-heart. A moment of clarity. A beat of silence. That emotional spacing gives the jokes more punch when they return. It also makes the world feel real, not just performative.

Comedy pacing is also about **escalation**. One of the most effective comic structures is the three-beat escalation: a setup, a callback, and then a heightening twist. A character tries something, fails, tries again, fails worse, tries a third time—and everything explodes. This rhythm keeps the audience leaning in. They recognize the pattern and want to see where it goes.

Ask ChatGPT for examples:

"Create a three-beat gag using the same setting but increasing absurdity."

Or:

"Write a scene that escalates a small argument into total chaos over three dialogue exchanges."

Another important rhythm tool: **pauses and silence**. Don't fear them. A pause before a punchline can make it land harder. A beat of awkward silence after a character says something outrageous can *be* the joke. Too many writers rush from joke to joke, forgetting that space is where the audience laughs. Comedy isn't wall-to-wall sound. It breathes.

Try prompting ChatGPT with:

"Insert strategic pauses into this comedic monologue to improve timing and emphasis."

Or:

"Rewrite this fast-paced scene to allow the jokes more room to land without dragging the momentum."

And don't forget **scene transitions**. The way you move from one scene to another affects pacing. A hard cut from chaos to stillness can be hilarious. A gentle dissolve after a gut-punch gag can let the audience breathe. How you end each scene affects how ready the viewer is for the next one. Pacing isn't just internal—it's cumulative. Every beat matters.

If your episode feels off, try printing the scene headings and reading them like a map. Where does it lag? Where does it spike? Where's the emotional beat? Where's the moment of pure comedy? If you can't find that balance, reshape the structure until it flows like music.

The ultimate goal? Your comedy should feel like a rhythm the audience gets pulled into. A song they recognize, even if they don't know what note is coming next. That rhythm is built by structure, trust, and letting the jokes *earn* their place.

So don't rush. Don't drag. Don't overfill. Let the scene land. Let the laugh breathe.

And when the timing's right?

Even a single word can bring the house down.

Dialogue That Snaps, Pops, and Surprises

In comedy, dialogue is the lightning rod. It's where character meets rhythm, where timing becomes a weapon, and where punchlines sneak up and detonate mid-scene. But great comedic dialogue isn't just about writing clever lines—it's about writing *the right lines*, in the right *voice*, at the right *moment*. It's about rhythm, specificity, contradiction, and tension. If your dialogue snaps, pops, and surprises, your scenes start to feel alive, electric, and deeply watchable—even before the next big joke hits.

Let's get one thing straight: **funny dialogue isn't realistic. It's hyper-real.** It's sharper, tighter, and faster than the way people actually speak—but still grounded in emotional truth. That's what gives it bite. You're distilling characters down to their most potent moments: the joke they'd only think of later in real life, the exact phrasing that reveals who they are, the pause that makes an ordinary line hilarious.

The first ingredient of snappy dialogue is **voice**. Every character needs a verbal fingerprint. What do they sound like? Do they talk fast? Are they precise or vague? Do they correct others, or never finish a sentence? Are they dramatic? Deadpan? Rambling? Nervous? Dialogue should *never* feel like it could be swapped between characters. Even if they're all reacting to the same situation, their tone and language should clash, not echo.

Use ChatGPT to test this:

"Write the same scene where three different characters explain why they missed a meeting—make sure each one sounds uniquely themselves."

Or:

"Create five different voices for characters reacting to the same awkward situation: being caught dancing alone in the break room."

Next is **rhythm**. Great comedic dialogue has musicality. It builds and releases tension. It uses repetition, interruption, escalation, and misdirection. Think about how a line *lands*—whether it snaps like a mousetrap or meanders into an unexpected beat. Short, punchy lines create speed and tension. Long, over-explained ones can build absurdity or awkwardness. The art is knowing when to switch gears.

Try ChatGPT with:

"Rewrite this flat dialogue so it builds rhythmically to a punchline using escalating logic."

Or:

"Give me examples of misdirection in dialogue—where the line starts one way and ends unexpectedly."

Don't underestimate the power of **silence and subtext**. Sometimes the funniest line is *no line at all.* A character saying "That's fine" through gritted teeth, followed by three seconds of silence, can hit harder than a page of overwritten jokes. Characters who say the opposite of what they feel, or who mask emotion with sarcasm or deadpan absurdity, often carry the most comic weight.

Great dialogue also surprises. It avoids cliché and defies expectation. Don't write the obvious response. If someone says, "You're acting crazy," don't have the other person say, "I'm not crazy." Have them say, "Good. Then the goat disguise is working." Comedy lives in left turns. You set up one idea—then swerve.

Use ChatGPT to practice:

"Write ten surprising punchlines to the line: 'This is a bad idea and you know it.'"

Or:

"Give me dialogue responses that flip the emotional tone mid-sentence for comedic effect."

Let's talk about **status**. In any scene, status is shifting. Who thinks they're in control? Who's losing it? Who's bluffing, deflecting, collapsing, or pretending they're fine? Comedy thrives on these tiny shifts. A low-status character trying to sound high-status is hilarious. A confident character getting rattled mid-monologue is even better. Your dialogue should reflect the power struggle *as it evolves.*

Try a prompt like:

"Write a scene between two co-workers where one slowly loses control of the conversation while trying to stay professional."

Another essential element: **callback and repetition**. When a line from earlier in the episode comes back later in a new form—or with a new meaning—it lands like a mini firework. It rewards the audience for paying attention. And it makes your script feel smart and cohesive without ever slowing down.

Use ChatGPT to generate possibilities:

"What are three ways a phrase like 'Not my circus' could be reused in an escalating comedy scene to get bigger laughs each time?"

Also remember that **dialogue reveals emotion indirectly**. A character doesn't need to say "I'm scared." They can say, "It's not that I'm worried, I just... alphabetized my canned goods in case I have to live in the basement for a year." That kind of sideways expression of emotion is not only funnier—it's more relatable. Comedy is often just anxiety in a better outfit.

To level up your scenes, try stripping dialogue down to the *essence*. Start with the emotional core—what does each character *want* in this moment? Then build the line around how they're failing to ask for it. That's where the humor lives: in the mismatch between need and behavior.

You can use ChatGPT like this:

"Write a scene where a character is desperate for comfort but disguises it by acting hyper-casual and uninterested."

Finally, **read your dialogue out loud**. Or better yet, have ChatGPT simulate a table read. Clunky lines, overwritten jokes, or uneven pacing become instantly obvious when spoken. Comedy is performance on the page. If it doesn't flow, it doesn't land. Fresh, snappy, surprising dialogue doesn't come from trying to be clever. It comes from knowing your characters so well that their words *can't* sound like anyone else's. It comes from playing with rhythm, undercutting emotion, and choosing honesty over formula. Your characters shouldn't sound like comedy writers. They should sound like themselves—funny, flawed, and fighting for something.

When you get it right, the jokes will feel effortless, the scenes will move like music, and the laughs will come from the characters—not just the lines.

Using ChatGPT to Create Hilarious Conversations

One of the best ways to supercharge your comedy writing is to collaborate with a partner who never sleeps, never runs out of ideas, and has a deep archive of jokes, rhythms, archetypes, and human behavior ready to go. That's where ChatGPT comes in. If you know how to use it well, it becomes your personal comedy room—a tireless, lightning-fast brainstorming buddy that can help you write dialogue, refine punchlines, and push your characters into funnier, fresher territory. And the beauty is, it's already trained to mimic tone, structure, and voice—all you need to do is steer.

So how do you use ChatGPT to create hilarious conversations? The key is to treat it like a writing partner who responds best to clarity and specifics. The more you give, the better it delivers. Start with **character setup**. Before asking for a scene, introduce your characters with tone, goals, and flaws. For example:

"One character is a self-serious therapist who thinks everything is a metaphor. The other is a literal-minded gym rat who only talks in workout metaphors. They're roommates arguing about what to cook for dinner."

Then, ask for a conversation based on that setup. You'll likely get a fast, functional scene with several jokes built in. But you don't have to stop there. You can now *refine*:

"Make the gym rat's metaphors even more ridiculous. Give the therapist a passive-aggressive tone."

"Punch up the ending with a visual gag involving protein powder."

"Rewrite the same conversation but escalate it into a heated competition over who can make the healthiest meal."

You can also use ChatGPT to write **conflict scenes**. Comedy lives in tension. Set up two opposing goals and ask the AI to generate a scene around them. For example:

"Character A is trying to confess their love. Character B thinks they're being asked to invest in a pyramid scheme. Write a miscommunication scene where both characters think they're on the same page—but clearly aren't."

To increase the fun, tell ChatGPT to build in **misdirection, callbacks, or escalating stakes**:

"Include a callback to an earlier conversation about beekeeping. Let the final line be the most absurd yet emotionally sincere."

"Each character should accidentally say something that sounds romantic—but is actually about finances."

If your dialogue is falling flat, ChatGPT can act as your **dialogue doctor**. Copy your scene into the prompt and ask:

"Make this scene 20% funnier without changing the core emotion."

"Rewrite this to build to a stronger punchline in the last three lines."

"Edit this so the characters talk over each other more and one keeps misunderstanding basic words."

For character voice, ask for **distinctive phrasing or verbal quirks**:

"Rewrite this character's dialogue so they speak in a hyper-formal tone but always mispronounce one big word per sentence."

"Make this character speak in motivational slogans even during serious conversations."

To experiment with **style and homage**, ask ChatGPT to rewrite a scene in the voice of a well-known show:

"Rewrite this roommate argument in the style of *Veep*—fast, angry, profane, and full of insults."

"Do a version of this breakup scene in the tone of *Fleabag*—dry, awkward, with direct-to-audience asides."

"Give me a scene in the style of *The Office*, with awkward silences, camera-aware glances, and painfully mundane stakes."

You can also write **alternate versions of the same scene** to test which is funniest:

"Give me three different takes on the same conversation: one dry and deadpan, one fast and silly, and one full of malapropisms and mixed metaphors."

"What's a version of this job interview scene where the applicant thinks it's a first date?"

ChatGPT is also brilliant for **creating setups that invite comedy**. Try:

"Give me ten conversation starters that sound polite but quickly lead to weird, uncomfortable, or wildly inappropriate places."

"Write a scene where two characters bond over something seemingly wholesome that quickly becomes dark or illegal."

And if you're stuck? Go meta:

"Write a scene about two comedy writers trying to write a scene and getting distracted by their own egos."

"Create a scene where a character tries to use ChatGPT to write a love letter but keeps getting weird results."

The best part? You're not married to any of it. You can mix, cut, riff, and rewrite. ChatGPT gives you a pile of creative clay—your job is to shape it into something with timing, tension, and a little weirdness that feels *like you*. Let the AI generate drafts, but keep your eye on the tone. Use it to explore rhythm, tweak punchlines, or brainstorm left-turns your own mind might've skipped.

In the end, hilarious conversations come from voice, tension, specificity, and surprise. ChatGPT can give you all of that—if you tell it who your characters are, what they're fighting about, and how far they're willing to go.

So pull up a blank page, give the setup, and let the dialogue fly. One laugh leads to the next, and your series starts writing itself—one hilarious exchange at a time.

Editing Jokes without Editing Out the Funny

Writing comedy is hard. Editing comedy is harder. It's where sharp becomes sharper—or gets sanded down into dull. You finally nail a funny scene, a great line, a brilliant bit of character banter—and then, in the name of pacing, clarity, or "tightening," you kill it. That's the danger: editing the joke so much it stops being funny. The trick is learning how to edit *for* laughs, not *against* them.

Editing in comedy is about rhythm, timing, clarity, and surprise. The goal isn't just to preserve the joke—it's to make sure the joke lands in the cleanest, most powerful way. It's about sculpting, not censoring. Cutting the excess without cutting the laugh. Let's walk through how to do that without gutting your voice—or your punchlines.

Start with this mindset: **jokes are not precious—but they are purposeful.** Every joke in your script should do one or more of the following:

- Reveal character
- Advance the story
- Build the world
- Escalate conflict
- Shift power
- Surprise the audience

If it doesn't do any of those things—even if it's funny—it might be fat. Good fat? Maybe. But maybe not. That's your call. Try highlighting each joke and asking: *What's this doing besides being funny?* If the answer is "nothing," then it has to be *really* funny to stay.

Use ChatGPT as your test reader:

"Here's a scene. Tell me which jokes feel earned and which ones feel like filler."

Or

"Help me rewrite this joke so it still hits but connects better to the character's motivation."

Now let's get surgical.

1. Trim the Setup

Most jokes die before the punchline because they take too long to get there. The audience doesn't laugh—they get lost. You want setups that are clean, visual, and emotionally clear. If you're setting up a misunderstanding, cut to the misinterpretation fast. If it's a wordplay joke, get the audience close to the edge—then push.

Ask ChatGPT:

"Rewrite this paragraph to get to the punchline quicker without losing the tone."

Or

"Shorten this joke setup to its most efficient version, keeping the rhythm intact."

2. Lose the Explainers

Don't explain the joke. Don't follow the punchline with "Get it?" Don't add a character repeating what just happened. If the joke doesn't land without explanation, either the setup's wrong, or the line's too clever for its own good. Let it hang. Let the silence work. Trust the audience.

3. Test Timing on the Page

Comedy is visual, but it's also about pacing on the page. A well-placed line break, ellipsis, or beat can give a punchline the pause it needs. Don't be afraid of space. Use rhythm in your formatting.

You can prompt ChatGPT to analyze flow:

"Where would you insert pauses or line breaks to improve comedic timing in this dialogue scene?"

4. Trim Redundant Jokes

A common trap is tagging the same beat multiple times. If a character says something funny, then another character repeats it, then a third says something similar—it gets old fast. Kill your weakest children. Keep the strongest beat. Let it stand alone and hit hard.

Try this:

"Here are three versions of the same joke. Which one is strongest, and why?"

Or

"Help me combine these overlapping jokes into one better version."

5. Punching Up, Not Piling On

If a joke is solid but not great, *punch it up*. Keep the structure, but play with the words, tone, or misdirection. Don't stack more jokes on top. Make the one you have better.

Ask ChatGPT:

"Rewrite this punchline to be sharper, more specific, or more surprising."

Or

"Give me five alt versions of this joke in different tones—dry, absurd, cruel, sincere, meta."

6. Mind the Character Voice

Sometimes a joke is funny—but not *for that person*. A shy character delivering a clever pun might feel off. A blunt realist using poetic irony? Doesn't track. When editing, make sure every joke *sounds* like it came from the character, not the writer.

Test it by asking:

"Would this line still be funny if said by another character? If yes, make it more specific to the original speaker's voice."

7. Preserve the Surprise

Great jokes work because of the twist—the unexpected word, the flipped logic, the wrong turn. If editing makes the punchline predictable, it dies. If it telegraphs the joke, it dies. Make sure the edit *tightens*, not telegraphs.

You can workshop surprise with ChatGPT:

"How can I rewrite this punchline so the last word flips the meaning more unexpectedly?"

8. Cut for Pace, Not Just Length

It's tempting to slice jokes just to get under page count. But don't cut the soul of the scene. Cut *around* the joke. Trim transitions, excess beats, unnecessary reactions. Protect what's truly funny—but let it breathe. Editing isn't about silence. It's about flow.

9. Read Aloud—Then Laugh (or Don't)

Always read comedy out loud. Hear the beat. Feel the rhythm. If it makes you smile silently, that's a maybe. If you actually laugh, it stays. If you think, "This should be funny," but you're not laughing—it probably needs work.

Ask ChatGPT:

"Simulate a table read of this scene. Who gets the biggest laugh? Where does it drag?"

Editing comedy is about trusting your taste, sharpening your aim, and cutting without fear. You're not trying to keep every laugh. You're trying to keep the *right* ones. You're turning a rough, funny draft into something tight, punchy, and alive—something that knows when to wink, when to whisper, and when to shout the perfect line at exactly the wrong moment.

Because the best comedies aren't written once. They're rewritten, tuned, tested, and stripped down until every joke shines like it was effortless.

Giving Each Episode a Strong Premise and Payoff

If comedy is the moment-to-moment laughter, then structure is the invisible backbone holding it all together. A great comedy episode doesn't just wander through bits—it *builds* something. It starts with a strong idea, tightens the tension, and lands with a payoff that's either hilarious, touching, or completely ridiculous (ideally all three). Without a strong premise and a satisfying payoff, even the funniest jokes feel like they're floating in a vacuum. With them, you've got something the audience will quote, revisit, and remember.

Let's start with what makes a **great comedic premise**: it's a simple, funny idea that creates natural tension and gives your characters room to reveal themselves. It doesn't need to be high-concept. It just needs to be loaded with comedic potential the moment it's stated.

Premise examples:

- Two friends accidentally join rival political campaigns and pretend they're not involved.
- A character tries to go an entire day without lying—and immediately realizes they lie constantly.
- Everyone forgets a co-worker's birthday... except one person, who overcompensates and makes it worse.

Each of these setups leads to inevitable complications. They create **a comic engine**—a question the episode is going to answer: *How far will these people go? Who will break first? What truth will emerge from the madness?*

Ask ChatGPT to help sharpen your ideas:

"Give me ten episode premises for a sitcom about roommates who all work night shifts and never see each other."

Or

"Rewrite this soft premise to make it funnier and more premise-driven."

Once you have the premise, develop the **comic tension**. This is where the characters' wants and flaws clash with the situation. Think about who's trying to control the story, who's resisting, and who's making things worse without realizing it. Good tension is character-driven. If your characters are just reacting to plot, the episode can feel thin. If they're driving the chaos with their own weirdness, the story becomes funnier and more grounded.

Now let's talk about the **payoff**. Every great comedy episode earns its laughs, but it also *lands* somewhere. The final scene or moment should be a twist, a resolution, a punchline, or an emotional beat that reflects or flips the original premise. You don't have to tie everything up—but the story should *resolve* the central tension in a surprising or poetic way.

Think about:

- Did the character change? Or double down on their flaw?
- Did the lie unravel? Or did the truth get buried under an even bigger one?
- Did they get what they wanted? Or learn they didn't need it?

Some classic types of comedic payoffs:

- **The Ironic Victory**: A character "wins" in a way that proves they've actually lost (e.g., they get the promotion,

but it means working weekends with their worst enemy).
- **The Circular Ending**: Everything goes back to exactly how it was—but now we know a little more.
- **The Bit That Comes Back**: A joke from the first scene returns in a new context, with a bigger laugh.
- **The Sweet Twist**: The comedy melts into something sincere—often the final 10 seconds.

Ask ChatGPT to generate variations:

"Give me five possible payoffs to a comedy episode where a character pretends to be an expert chef and gets trapped catering a real wedding."

Or

"Suggest endings for an episode where a character hides a minor injury that keeps getting worse."

A few more tools to keep your episode structure tight:

1. Keep the A Story Clean

The A story should carry the main premise and build steadily. Subplots are great, but they should *echo*, contrast, or heighten the A story—not distract from it. If you're juggling too many stories, trim down.

2. Use Escalation

Your episode should build. Each scene adds tension or raises stakes. If your premise is "someone tells a lie," the story isn't about the lie—it's about what that lie *forces them to do next*. Let the situation spiral.

3. Make the Ending Feel Inevitable, Yet Surprising

The best endings feel like they couldn't have gone any other way—but also catch the audience off guard. You build toward something, then twist it one last time.

Ask ChatGPT to test this:

"Does this ending feel earned based on the premise? If not, how could it better reflect the arc of the episode?"

4. Stay Thematically Consistent

Even a goofy episode should reflect your show's core themes. If your show is about self-delusion, your ending shouldn't be a clean moral lesson—it should be a deeper delusion. If your show is about identity, your ending might push a character into a funnier, more confused version of themselves.

5. Leave the Audience with a Button

The button is that final joke, visual gag, or one-liner that gives the audience a satisfying emotional rhythm. It's the last flavor in the mouth. You can plant it early in the episode and bring it back, or surprise everyone with something totally new.

When you get the premise and payoff right, the episode doesn't just work—it *sings*. The jokes have context. The story has purpose. And the characters feel like they've taken a ridiculous, emotionally real journey... even if it all started with a stolen sandwich.

So use ChatGPT to brainstorm, escalate, and experiment. Test different endings. Build alternate versions of the same setup. See what pushes the characters into better trouble. Don't just write funny scenes—write *episodes with a pulse.*

Writing Tag Scenes, Cold Opens, and Cliffhangers

Not every laugh lives in the body of an episode. Some sneak in before the theme song even plays. Others linger in the final seconds, leaving the audience with a smirk, a twist, or a stunned silence. That's the job of cold opens, tag scenes, and cliffhangers. These brief, often overlooked parts of an episode do more than fill time—they create lasting impressions, set the tone, deepen the world, and in some cases, keep your audience watching all night long.

Let's break down how each one works—and how to make them funny, sharp, and loaded with character energy.

Cold Opens: The First Laugh Before the Plot Begins

The cold open is the comedy appetizer. It comes before the title or credits and exists *outside* the main story. It doesn't need to advance the plot, but it *does* need to announce the show's voice. Think of it as a teaser for your tone: "This is the kind of world you've stepped into. Stick around."

Some classic cold open structures:

- **Mini-Sketch**: A self-contained, unrelated moment of absurdity (e.g., *The Office*'s fire drill or stapler-in-Jell-O).
- **Character Bit**: A spotlight moment that distills a character's personality into a single behavior (e.g., someone practicing their Oscar speech while doing laundry).
- **Running Gag Setup**: Introduce a visual or verbal bit that'll echo later in the episode.
- **Misdirection**: Begin with a dramatic setup that flips into something totally mundane or ridiculous.

To write a strong cold open:

1. **Get in fast**—no exposition, no setup.
2. **Land one clear beat**—don't try to squeeze in a subplot.
3. **Exit strong**—a final line, expression, or image that makes the title card feel earned.

Use ChatGPT to generate:

"Give me five cold open ideas for a comedy about an overworked emergency room staff with too much downtime."

Or

"Write a cold open that begins like a bank robbery but ends with a group therapy session for shoplifters."

Tag Scenes: The Final Chuckle or Callback

Tag scenes happen after the episode's main story wraps up. They're short—usually 30 seconds to a minute—and serve as a comedic grace note. Where the cold open sets the tone, the tag scene *reaffirms it*. It's not just an afterthought—it's the punctuation mark.

Common tag scene types:

- **Callback Tag**: Refer to a joke or event from earlier in the episode and take it one step further.
- **Mini Fallout**: Show the short-term consequences of a character's decision after the credits roll.

- **Visual Bit**: A wordless or physical gag that adds one last laugh.
- **Alt Angle**: Return to a background character or subplot that got interrupted earlier.

Tips for writing a tag:

- Let it feel like a reward for people who watched closely.
- Avoid new story beats—this is dessert, not a second dinner.
- Go out on a beat that deepens character or makes the world feel bigger.

Ask ChatGPT for ideas like:

"Give me tag scene ideas for an episode where two characters faked being lawyers and won a case by accident."

Or

"Write a 30-second tag where a character tries to return a goat to the wrong apartment."

Cliffhangers: The Comedy Version of "Wait, What?"

Cliffhangers are usually associated with drama—but they're just as powerful in comedy, especially if your show has a season arc or serialized elements. A great comedic cliffhanger leaves the audience gasping *and* laughing.

You don't need explosions or plot twists. Sometimes the best cliffhangers are:

- **A ridiculous reveal**: "Wait... you're my *what*?"
- **A new complication**: "The boss is coming back? I thought we buried her!"
- **A perfectly timed interruption**: A proposal, a secret, or a breakdown mid-sentence.
- **A visual gag with consequences**: Opening the door to reveal... 300 ferrets.

Tips for comedy cliffhangers:

1. **Let the reveal be character-driven**—not just random chaos.
2. **Use silence or shock** to sell the surprise. Then cut.
3. **Let the setup be clean and visual**, so the audience finishes the moment in their own head.

Try ChatGPT prompts like:

"Write three comedic cliffhangers that could end a workplace comedy episode about office rivalries."

Or

"What's a funny last-second twist in a romance subplot between two highly incompatible characters?"

Putting It All Together

Cold opens hook. Tag scenes seal. Cliffhangers linger.

When used together, these small moments add tremendous flavor and flow to your episodes. They frame the comedy. They stretch the world. They make your series feel confident, alive, and *bingeable*. They're not filler—they're rhythm. If you use them intentionally, your episodes won't just be funny. They'll *stick*.

So whether you're writing a fake funeral gone wrong or a romantic misunderstanding that ends in public karaoke, take an extra minute to ask:

What's the funniest way into this?

What's the funniest way out?

And what's the one line that makes people need to see what happens next?

Structuring a Season of Comedy with Mini-Arcs

When you're building a comedy series, you're not just writing episodes—you're crafting a whole season that breathes, evolves, and holds together like a song. Even if your show is mostly episodic, the strongest comedies structure their seasons around *mini-arcs*—short bursts of story, relationship tension, or character growth that run for two to four episodes at a time. These arcs give your season momentum. They keep it from feeling like a gag reel. They let jokes build, pay off, and echo back with new meaning.

So how do you structure a season of comedy using mini-arcs?

Start by imagining your season not as one long arc, but as a **series of waves**. Each wave builds, breaks, and resets. Some waves are emotional (a character trying to get over an ex). Some are plot-based (a secret relationship, a new job, a lie that snowballs). Some are thematic (everyone in the group dealing with change in different ways). Each wave lasts a few episodes, overlaps with others, and lets you deepen the characters without losing the laughs.

Let's break this down into a simple rhythm:

1. Establishing the World (Episodes 1–3)

You're setting the tone, voice, premise, and core relationships. The pilot introduces the protagonist's want or flaw. The next two episodes deepen the group dynamics, escalate one conflict, and maybe introduce a running gag or antagonist.

Mini-arc example:

- A new employee joins the office and causes chaos.
- One character is secretly living in the storage closet.
- Someone gets dumped and swears they're "totally fine" (they're not).

You can ask ChatGPT:

"Give me a three-episode character arc that introduces a lovable but deeply inappropriate boss figure."

2. Shifting the Status Quo (Episodes 4–6)

Now that the audience knows the rules of the world, you break them a little. Introduce a challenge, shake up a dynamic, or give a character a temporary win that backfires.

Mini-arc example:

- The gang forms a band and gets one gig... which goes terribly.
- Two characters fake a relationship for social or professional reasons.
- A recurring side character suddenly becomes a real threat.

This arc gives mid-season energy and tests the group.

Use ChatGPT to help:

"Create a mid-season mini-arc where a rivalry between two characters escalates until it's interrupted by an unexpected crisis."

3. Emotional Undercurrents (Episodes 7–9)

This is the quietest stretch, where you let something real surface. The jokes don't stop—but there's room for vulnerability, change, or tension. You might dip into backstory or set up future fallout.

Mini-arc example:

- One character gets promoted and slowly drifts from the group.
- Someone's parent visits, revealing long-suppressed insecurities.
- A secret finally comes out... but not to the person it matters to.

Let ChatGPT explore tone:

"Write a three-episode outline for a comedy series where the main character pretends to be confident but starts unraveling."

4. Chaos and Collisions (Episodes 10–12)

This is your escalation arc. Let everything simmered so far hit the fan. Storylines collide. Misunderstandings build. Characters make decisions they'll soon regret—or that finally push them forward.

Mini-arc example:

- A romantic subplot explodes at the worst possible moment.
- A lie gets exposed in front of everyone.
- The main character is forced into a leadership role they're unqualified for.

Ask ChatGPT:

"Build a chaos arc for a workplace comedy where three characters lie about the same thing and it all unravels during a company retreat."

5. Season Climax and Reset (Episodes 13–14)

You don't need a happy ending—but you do need a *landing*. Your characters don't have to grow a lot. Maybe they grow *a little*. Maybe they don't grow at all, but something shifts—just enough to keep the story alive for next season.

Use payoffs:

- Bring back a joke from Episode 2 with new context.
- Let the character who always bails out actually show up.
- Let the chaos calm *just enough* to reset the board.

Mini-arc example:

- The gang tries to keep a big secret from one character... who already knows.

- A promotion or move threatens to split the group.
- Everyone's forced into therapy and pretends it didn't work (but it did, a little).

Let ChatGPT generate options:

"Outline a two-part finale arc for a comedy about four broke friends trying to start a business out of their apartment."

Tips for Great Comedy Season Arcs

- **Anchor each mini-arc in character.** Even if the plot is ridiculous, the emotional core should track. Ask yourself: what does this arc *mean* for this person?
- **Overlap arcs.** While one arc is peaking, another can begin. This overlap keeps episodes rich and dynamic.
- **Let running gags evolve.** A simple line or prop from episode one can become a huge payoff in episode ten.
- **Build reversals.** Let power, emotion, or perspective shift across arcs. A character who's always in control loses it. Someone who's the joke becomes the hero—just once.

When you structure your season with mini-arcs, your show feels like it has movement *without ever abandoning the funny*. The audience gets attached, not just entertained. They binge because they care—and because every three or four episodes, something *shifts*.

So go ahead and map out those arcs. Use ChatGPT to fill in the beats. Write episodes that feed each other. Let the laughter carry the story—and let the story deepen the laughs.

Introducing Recurring Gags and Catchphrases

Recurring gags and catchphrases are the secret sauce that turns a good comedy series into a *beloved* one. They're the moments audiences quote back at you. They're the inside jokes that make a show feel like a shared experience. But these tools aren't just about repetition—they're about rhythm, timing, character, and escalation. When done right, recurring gags and catchphrases become emotional shorthand and comedy fuel. When done wrong, they feel lazy, forced, or like filler.

So how do you create running jokes and catchphrases that land every time without wearing out their welcome?

Let's start with **why** they work. The truth is, audiences love patterns. We're wired to recognize them, anticipate them, and feel satisfaction when the pattern pays off—especially when it returns with a twist. A well-placed gag isn't just a repeat. It's a *callback* with deeper resonance. It rewards loyal viewers and invites casual ones into the club. It also helps build the identity of your show. If someone hears a phrase out of context and knows exactly which show it's from, you've done your job.

The key is to root every recurring bit in **character**. A catchphrase shouldn't be random. It should reflect someone's worldview, emotional defense mechanism, delusion, or quirk. Think "No soup for you!" in *Seinfeld*, "Treat yo' self" in *Parks and Recreation*, or "Cool, cool, cool... no doubt, no doubt" from *Brooklyn Nine-Nine*. These phrases aren't just lines—they *are* the character.

Use ChatGPT to help you generate character-specific catchphrases:

"Create five possible catchphrases for a character who's always trying to sound calm while spiraling internally."

Or

"Give me recurring expressions for a character who thinks they're a genius but keeps misunderstanding everything."

Running gags, on the other hand, are behavior-based. They're jokes that play out over time, often without being directly called out. Some are visual (a character always enters through the wrong door). Some are situational (someone always fakes an emergency to avoid conflict). Some are relational (a character tries to bond with someone who clearly dislikes them). The trick is that the *repetition makes it funnier*, not stale—*because the context changes*. The world moves forward, but the gag stays hilariously stuck.

Try this with ChatGPT:

"Give me three recurring gag ideas for a character who's always accidentally overhearing the wrong part of a conversation."

Or

"Write a series of three escalating versions of a recurring gag about someone who refuses to admit they're lost."

Tips for Creating Effective Catchphrases

1. **Make them short and rhythmically punchy.**
   A good catchphrase fits in one breath. It's sticky. It has internal music. Bonus points if it uses unusual words or

strange cadence. Something that *sounds* like no one else.

2. **Use contradiction.**
   Catchphrases often work because they reveal the *opposite* of what's true. "I got this" from someone who never does. "Everything's fine" from someone clearly on fire. The disconnect is the joke.
3. **Give it context before you repeat it.**
   Let the first time feel earned. Don't write a catchphrase for a character who hasn't earned the moment. Use it in a moment of tension or revelation, then repeat it when the stakes are lower—or higher. That's how it becomes funny on multiple levels.
4. **Don't overuse it.**
   Frequency matters. A great catchphrase appears just enough to feel like a signature, not a crutch. Use it when the rhythm of the story calls for it, not every time the character speaks.
5. **Let it evolve.**
   A catchphrase that changes slightly every time can stay fresh longer. Maybe the phrase gets misused by others. Maybe a rival starts mocking it. Maybe it shows up in a wildly inappropriate context. That shifting echo builds humor and keeps it from getting stale.

You can play with ChatGPT here too:

"Give me five alternate versions of a catchphrase that starts as 'Don't look at me like that' and gets increasingly dramatic."

Or

"Write a scene where a catchphrase is misused by another character, creating tension or comedy."

Tips for Sustaining a Running Gag

- **Let the audience notice it before the characters do.**
  When a gag becomes part of the background—until someone finally points it out—it becomes even funnier.
- **Escalate.**
  The best recurring gags don't just repeat—they grow. Maybe the gag gets the character into deeper trouble. Maybe it starts affecting other characters. That amplification keeps it alive.
- **Break the pattern—for effect.**
  Sometimes the absence of the gag is the joke. Maybe the catchphrase is replaced by silence. Maybe the expected behavior doesn't happen... and everyone feels weird. That subversion adds dimension.

ChatGPT can help escalate:

"Write three versions of a gag where a character always gives way too much personal information in group meetings—and eventually gets called out for it."

Or

"Create a visual running gag involving a malfunctioning office item that becomes a source of superstition."

Final Thought: The Emotional Payoff

Sometimes the biggest laughs come when the joke we've been laughing at for twelve episodes suddenly hits an emotional note. Maybe the catchphrase shows up in a vulnerable moment. Maybe a character uses it to comfort someone instead of deflecting. Comedy and heart can share the same sentence—and that's when a line becomes iconic.

So don't chase the gag. Build it. Seed it. Let it grow in the weird, wonderful soil of your characters and their flaws.

Because when the right line returns at the perfect moment—it's not just funny.

It's unforgettable.

Using Absurdity and Exaggeration without Losing Grounding

Absurdity and exaggeration are powerful tools in comedy—they're what let a character fight a goose in a courtroom or stage a wedding to win a bet about emotional vulnerability. They're what turn an average day into a spiralling farce, what allow your show to live just a few inches to the left of reality. But with great ridiculousness comes great responsibility. Push too far, and your comedy unravels into nonsense. Keep it grounded, and absurdity becomes rocket fuel.

So how do you write wild, heightened, laugh-out-loud situations without breaking the emotional backbone of your story or losing your audience?

The secret is **anchoring the absurd in something true**. Characters can do outrageous things, but their *motives*—what drives them to those things—have to come from recognizable human emotion. The goose fight works because the character can't admit they're afraid of confrontation. The staged wedding works because someone's desperate to prove they're lovable. The more honest the emotional engine, the further the comedy can fly.

Start with the emotional truth:

- What's the character afraid of?
- What are they trying to avoid or win?
- What's at stake *for them*, even if the situation is ridiculous?

You can use ChatGPT to play with this balance:

"Create an absurd scene where a character runs for mayor of their apartment building, but make their motivation heartbreakingly sincere."

Or

"Give me five over-the-top ideas rooted in characters trying to avoid difficult conversations."

Absurdity works best when it's **situational**, not arbitrary. The world needs rules—even if they're weird. Think of *The Good Place*, where the afterlife has frozen yogurt shops and flying shrimp—but operates on a tightly constructed system of moral points. Or *Brooklyn Nine-Nine*, where a man builds a full heist plot every Halloween, but still has to clock in and report to HR.

Ask: *What's possible in your world?* Then: *What's not?*

Use ChatGPT to define those limits:

"List ten absurd rules for a fictional workplace that still has to meet normal government regulations."

Or

"What are some funny consequences for breaking minor rules in an otherwise grounded world?"

The best absurd comedy also relies on **characters taking it seriously**. The more ridiculous the situation, the more your characters need to commit to it. They don't wink at the audience or stop to say, "This is nuts." They go all-in. That commitment sells the joke. Let your characters bring their real anxieties, neuroses, and blind spots into the madness. Let them argue about the *ethics* of hypnotizing a dog or the *morality* of competitive speed hugging.

You can explore this dynamic with prompts like:

"Write a scene where two characters argue passionately about the fairness of a spoon-only dinner party."

Or

"Create a debate between co-workers over whether someone's imaginary friend should be included in a staff vote."

Visual absurdity also plays a big role. Think of strange props, costumes, signage, or background action that heightens the world without distracting from it. A cluttered break room with signs like *"No Crying in Front of the Microwave"*. A character who always brings a parrot to meetings. Let the visual absurdity reflect the emotional state of the world. Don't overuse it—one strong visual gag often lands better than five weak ones.

Let ChatGPT brainstorm for you:

"Give me visual background gags for a comedy set in a failing coworking space."

Or

"What are some funny, increasingly absurd protest signs for a character who's mad about trivial inconveniences?"

Another technique: **escalation with logic**. Absurdity doesn't have to be random—it can be the *logical conclusion of flawed logic*. If someone believes one lie, what's the natural next step? If they fake being a priest to impress someone, what happens when they get asked to officiate a funeral? Start grounded. Let each beat build on the last. The heightening makes the absurdity feel earned.

Ask ChatGPT:

"Write a step-by-step comic escalation of a lie about knowing karate that ends in a full dojo showdown."

Or

"Create a progression where a character fakes being allergic to technology and ends up leading an anti-wi-fi cult."

And here's where grounding comes back in: **end with impact**. Even in the most absurd situations, try to land your episode or scene with an emotional beat that feels real. The chaos might not resolve—but the characters should come away having learned, lost, or revealed something true. That final tug grounds the experience. It reminds the audience that these people *feel real*, even when everything else feels like a fever dream.

Examples of grounded endings after absurd plots:

- A character who spent the episode in a bear costume realizes no one noticed—and quietly hangs it up.
- After staging a fake break-in, two roommates admit they're terrified of living alone.
- A rival prank war ends not with a win, but with one character saying, "This was the most fun I've had in months."

Ask ChatGPT for emotional resonance:

"Give me ten emotional truths a character might reveal after participating in something absurd."

Or

"Suggest quiet closing moments for a chaotic episode that let the audience feel something honest."

Absurdity isn't about being random. It's about pushing reality just far enough that we can laugh at what we'd never dare do ourselves. When paired with emotional truth, consistent logic, and character clarity, it becomes one of the most effective comedic tools you've got.

So go weird. Go wild. Just make sure your characters care deeply—*too* deeply—about whatever ridiculous thing they're doing.

Satire, Spoof, and Social Commentary in Comedy

Comedy isn't just for punchlines—it's also one of the sharpest tools for saying something real. Through satire, spoof, and commentary, comedy can expose hypocrisy, challenge power, and hold a mirror up to society's strangest habits. The best part? You get to do all that while making people laugh. It's the spoonful of sugar that helps the truth go down—but it only works when the humor lands first, and the message is baked into the cake, not frosted on top.

Let's start with **satire**, the art of exaggerating real ideas, behaviors, or institutions to reveal their flaws. Satire isn't just "look how dumb this is"—it's "look how *normal* we've made something ridiculous." It works best when it comes from a point of view. Think of *Veep*'s political chaos, *The Colbert Report*'s right-wing character parody, or *South Park*'s equal-opportunity mockery of culture, politics, and human absurdity. The laughs come from truth, bent just enough to sting.

To write satire, you first need a **target**. Not a person, but a behavior, belief, or system. What do you find absurd? What do your characters accept without questioning? That's your entry point. Then, **exaggerate the logic** of that idea until it collapses under its own weight. If you're satirizing social media clout, maybe your characters join a fake cult just to boost their follower count. If you're targeting corporate jargon, maybe no one in the company remembers what the product even is—but they're all terrified of being the first to admit it.

Ask ChatGPT to build out satire like:

"Create a satirical premise about wellness culture taken to a bizarre extreme."

Or

"Write a character who perfectly satirizes startup CEOs using exaggerated but grounded dialogue."

Now let's look at **spoof**, which is comedy's love letter to genre—with a wink and a gut punch. Spoof mocks the rules of a specific type of story, often by exaggerating tropes or flipping expectations. Think of *Airplane!*, *Scary Movie*, or *Popstar: Never Stop Never Stopping*. A good spoof doesn't just make fun of the surface. It understands what makes the original tick—and then blows it up.

The trick with spoof is **specificity**. Don't just parody "horror" or "action." Parody *this kind* of horror—the over-serious, slow-burn kind with cryptic symbols and dream sequences. Then exaggerate the pacing, make the metaphors way too literal, or show what it's like to be the one normal person in a genre that's completely lost its mind.

Use ChatGPT to play with it:

"Write a spoof of prestige true-crime documentaries that focuses on a stolen sandwich."

Or

"Create dialogue for a parody of overly dramatic courtroom scenes where the judge won't stop crying."

Spoof works great when it's paired with **genre-savvy characters**—people who are aware of the clichés and call them out or lean into them. This lets you mix spoof with actual character development. Your detective might realize they've been following a trope script their whole life—and decide to break the pattern.

Now let's talk **social commentary**, which doesn't have to be loud, edgy, or political to be effective. Comedy is commentary any time it draws attention to something broken, weird, or overlooked. It can be personal, cultural, or societal. Maybe your show mocks dating app culture by showing someone swiping at funerals. Maybe it explores 'workaholism' through a character who literally can't stop giving motivational speeches, even in a hospital bed.

The key to strong commentary? **Show the behavior, don't explain it.** Let your characters live inside the system you're mocking, then watch how it traps, shapes, or breaks them. Use the form itself—like a workplace sitcom, mockumentary, or rom-com structure—to reflect the problem. And above all, **stay funny first**. If the message takes over, it becomes a sermon. If the joke *is* the message, it hits harder and lasts longer.

Ask ChatGPT to dig deeper:

"Give me three ways to explore toxic productivity culture through comedic character arcs."

Or

"Write a scene where a character delivers an emotional speech that accidentally becomes scathing social commentary on influencer life."

Blending the Three

Many great comedies use satire, spoof, and commentary at once:

- *The Simpsons* satirizes suburban life, spoofs genre conventions, and comments on politics—all in a single episode.
- *Community* turns every episode into a genre spoof while making smart points about ego, trauma, and identity.
- *The Rehearsal* (Nathan Fielder's work) is surreal satire mixed with social experiment and commentary on human control and connection.

If you're writing your own series, you can build arcs where:

- A recurring spoof element escalates into satire (*e.g., a parody of cooking shows that turns into commentary on class*).
- Satirical exaggeration pays off emotionally (*e.g., a corporate drone discovers self-worth by rebelling against nonsense metrics*).
- A background gag becomes a pointed social critique (*e.g., an "emotional support intern" becomes company policy*).

Use ChatGPT to outline long-game ideas:

"Design a season arc that spoofs reality TV while satirizing the way people commodify emotions online."

Or

"Create a subplot that seems like a joke at first but becomes a surprisingly layered commentary on fame."

Comedy that says something isn't preachy—it's *pointed.* It asks, "What are we doing?" and "Why is that considered normal?" It uses exaggeration to clarify, not distract. The more truth you find under the joke, the louder the laugh—and the longer it echoes after the credits roll.

So go ahead. Be bold. Be absurd. Be sharp. Whether you're mocking billionaires launching space cults or poking holes in public transit etiquette, your show can be funny *and* smart, silly *and* scathing.

Writing Comedy about Serious Things (and Not Making It Cringe)

Writing comedy about serious things is like dancing on a tightrope in clown shoes—you might make them laugh, but one wrong step and you're the punchline. Done well, it's profound. Done badly, it's awkward, tone-deaf, or downright painful to watch. So how do you tackle tough subjects—grief, trauma, addiction, mental health, identity, injustice—without minimizing them, sensationalizing them, or making your audience wince and whisper, "Too soon"?

The answer is both simple and challenging: **respect the truth, but don't flinch from the comedy**. It's not about making light of serious things. It's about shining light *through* them.

Comedy is often how people cope. It's a survival tool. It helps us process the things that don't make sense. When you write comedy about serious subjects, you're not mocking the pain—you're revealing the absurdity, humanity, and contradictions *within* it.

Let's start with a foundational rule: **you're not writing about a subject—you're writing about people going through it**. The closer your comedy stays to character, the more room you have to explore hard truths. You don't make fun of grief. You show someone trying to fold a fitted sheet while processing a funeral. You don't mock mental illness. You show a character obsessively color-coding their spice rack because it's the one thing they *can* control. The humor doesn't come from the issue—it comes from the behavior.

Use ChatGPT to help you ground tough topics:

"Write a scene where a character processes a breakup by giving unsolicited relationship advice to strangers at a dog park."

Or

"Give me three comic situations where a character dealing with anxiety tries to act like a motivational speaker."

Another key to avoiding cringe is **tone control**. Serious-comedy doesn't mean bouncing between a death scene and a fart joke. It's about finding *one tone* that can hold emotional tension and humor without yanking the audience back and forth. Think of *Fleabag*, *BoJack Horseman*, *Ramy*, or *After Life*. These shows walk into heavy territory but carry emotional integrity and comedic honesty the entire way.

To test your tone, ask:

- *Is the joke punching down?* If yes, cut it.
- *Is the joke undermining or avoiding the emotional moment?* Then rework it.
- *Is the joke heightening the emotional truth by revealing how people behave under pressure?* That's gold.

You can explore this with ChatGPT:

"Rewrite this dramatic scene to include humor that adds emotional depth, not distraction."

Or

"Insert a character reaction that deflects sadness with awkward, overly formal behavior."

Also essential: **context and timing.** You can joke about anything *if* the story has earned it. A joke about death five minutes into a pilot hits differently than one 10 episodes into a season where we know the characters, the loss, and the emotional stakes. The more real the setup, the more effective the release. Don't start with the gag—start with the emotional truth, then layer in the coping behavior, the distraction, the accidental awkwardness that makes it human *and* funny.

Here's a helpful prompt:

"What's a moment of comedy that can happen at a serious event (like a funeral or intervention) that doesn't undercut the gravity of the moment?"

Or

"Write a scene where two characters argue about grief while doing something totally mundane—like trying to build a bookshelf."

Another powerful technique is **comic contradiction.** Comedy thrives on contrast. A character trying to act fine when they're clearly not. A hospital scene where the beep of a heart monitor plays a recognizable song. A support group where the snacks keep getting more absurd. These aren't disrespectful—they're *human.* When real pain meets real absurdity, comedy often shows up.

What you want to avoid is **joking *at* the issue** rather than **joking *through* it.** It's not funny to make fun of trauma. It's incredibly funny to watch someone use sarcasm, bravado, or ill-timed advice as armor against what they're feeling. That's what makes it resonate. That's what makes it powerful.

Let ChatGPT explore contradictions:

"Create a character who uses business metaphors to talk about their divorce and doesn't realize how inappropriate it sounds."

Or

"Write a scene where a character tries to fire their therapist before accidentally having a breakthrough mid-sentence."

Here's the final and maybe most important rule: **you don't need a clean resolution.** When writing serious comedy, don't feel like you have to wrap it up with a hug or a moral. Sometimes the most honest ending is a character laughing through tears, or sitting in awkward silence, or saying something totally inappropriate and being forgiven anyway. Life is messy. Let your comedy reflect that.

When you let the humor live *inside* the pain—when your jokes come from emotional honesty rather than deflection—you don't just avoid cringe. You hit something beautiful. You write a moment someone out there recognizes in their own life and thinks, *finally—someone gets it.*

So yes, write about death, loss, shame, fear, identity, illness, heartbreak, and injustice.

Just make sure your characters are still trying, still failing, and still making wildly inappropriate jokes to get through the day.

Cultural Humor vs. Universal Humor

Comedy can be a passport or a mirror. It can take audiences into a world they've never experienced—or show them something they've known their whole lives, but funnier. That's the dynamic between cultural humor and universal humor. One is rooted in specific customs, dialects, behaviors, and norms. The other taps into shared human experiences—awkwardness, fear, ego, love, embarrassment. Both are powerful. The real magic happens when you blend the two—letting your audience laugh because they relate *or* because they're learning something new.

So how do you balance cultural humor with universal appeal in your comedy series?

Cultural Humor: Specific, Sharp, and Grounded in Truth

Cultural humor draws from identity: ethnicity, religion, region, generation, language, family structure, food, politics, and more. It's not just about references—it's about rhythms, expectations, habits, and contradictions within a community. It shows up in how people argue, celebrate, avoid confrontation, overcompensate, or parent.

Think of shows like *Ramy*, *Kim's Convenience*, *Black-ish*, *Reservation Dogs*, or *Derry Girls*. The comedy is rich with specificity—accents, rituals, mispronunciations, intergenerational clashes, slang, food metaphors—but the stories still connect because the underlying dynamics are familiar: wanting approval, needing independence, being torn between old and new worlds.

The key to writing good cultural humor is **honesty over stereotype**. You're not writing *about* a culture from the outside—you're writing *within* it. If a joke could apply to any group, it's not cultural humor—it's generic. If the joke comes from inside a contradiction, fear, or truth that's lived, it's gold.

Use ChatGPT to explore nuance like:

"Write a scene between a second-generation immigrant and their parent arguing about the pronunciation of a dish, but make it about respect and identity underneath."

Or

"Give me five subtle, character-based jokes about generational gaps within a traditional family setting."

Cultural humor is especially powerful when the characters *don't realize* they're being funny. The son translating something wrong on purpose. The aunt who guilt-trips using mystical sayings. The neighbor who shows up at midnight because "you still haven't tasted my stew." These aren't bits—they're truth.

Universal Humor: Broad, Relatable, and Emotional

Universal humor isn't about watering down. It's about tapping into things *everyone* feels. It's the roommate who never cleans. The co-worker who steals your idea. The ex who texts at midnight. It's physical awkwardness, failed flirting, bad advice, overconfidence, denial, self-sabotage, pretending you're fine when you're obviously not. It's *why people laugh in the dark*.

Universal humor is essential for grounding your story. If your cultural moments are the flavor, the universal moments are the emotional foundation. They let the audience say, "I've been there," even if they've never been in that country, home, or church.

You can practice this with prompts like:

"Write a scene where a character avoids confrontation by doing something absurdly polite—make it culturally specific, but emotionally universal."

Or

"Give me five moments of physical comedy that could happen in any country and still land."

Great universal humor works *without translation* because it plays off basic instincts: jealousy, pride, fear, love. It's what makes silent comedies, like those of Chaplin or Mr. Bean, still land around the world. The emotion drives the laugh.

Blending the Two

Here's where the real power lies—using cultural specifics to deliver universal truths. A deeply particular moment becomes global *because* it's so richly personal. The funnier and more rooted the situation, the more everyone connects. Not despite the culture, but because they see themselves *through* it.

For example:

- A bar mitzvah that spirals into chaos because of family politics? That's Jewish culture *and* universal adolescence anxiety.
- A hijab-wearing teen trying to hide a hickey? That's culturally specific *and* about the awkwardness of growing up.
- A grandma who cures everything with herbs and curses the neighbors? That's rooted in old-world traditions, but speaks to the power of belief, guilt, and love.

Use ChatGPT to hybridize:

"Create a comedic misunderstanding rooted in a specific cultural practice, but with emotional stakes that anyone could relate to."

Or

"Write a joke that begins with a culturally specific setup but ends on a universally relatable punchline about disappointment."

Avoiding the Pitfalls

There are two big traps here:

1. **Overgeneralization** – trying to write "for everyone" and ending up with jokes that feel bland, vague, or fake.
2. **Over-insularity** – writing jokes so specific that they require an explainer or alienate the audience.

The way through is **context and character.** If a joke needs cultural knowledge, don't avoid it—just *layer it in with clarity*. The audience should get the *emotion*, even if they don't get every reference. And those who *do* get the reference? They'll love you forever.

Try this with ChatGPT:

"Write a culturally specific scene that works on two levels—funny for outsiders, deeply layered for insiders."

Or

"Suggest character actions that reflect cultural norms without needing a line of explanation."

Cultural humor says, "This is who we are."

Universal humor says, "This is who we *all* are."

When they meet, your comedy resonates across borders, languages, and timelines.

So don't dilute your world to be understood. Sharpen it. Populate it with characters who are *of* somewhere—but who feel everything we all do: shame, pride, confusion, jealousy, joy, hunger, and hope.

Your job is not to write for everyone. It's to write **honestly enough** that everyone *recognizes* themselves—even in someone completely different.

Designing Iconic Comedy Scenes with AI Visualization

Some comedy scenes are so vivid, they become etched in the audience's memory forever. Think Lucy and the chocolates on the conveyor belt. Think Dwight Schrute in a fire drill. Think Fleabag's silent dinner table confession moment, or the fight in *Bridesmaids* over who's the better maid of honor. These scenes are more than funny—they're *iconic*. Not just because of the writing, but because of how the comedy unfolds visually. And today, with the help of AI, you can begin *seeing* your scenes before they're even shot—designing your comedy for maximum impact, rhythm, and memorability.

Let's talk about how to do that.

The Anatomy of an Iconic Comedy Scene

A great comedy scene doesn't just deliver laughs. It creates a moment where story, character, timing, and visual absurdity come together in one unforgettable setup. That's where visualization comes in. Before production. Before casting. Even before final script lock—you can now use AI to storyboard, mock-up, or sketch out your scenes.

But it all starts with **intention**. Ask yourself:

- *What is the emotional tension underneath this scene?*
- *What's the power dynamic between the characters?*
- *What's the image the audience will remember even if they forget the dialogue?*

An iconic scene usually has:

- **A clear central conflict** (someone wants something, and someone's in the way)
- **A strong visual anchor** (a setting, prop, or absurd physical action)
- **Escalation** (the situation spirals)
- **A payoff or reversal** (something flips, breaks, or lands unexpectedly)

Using ChatGPT to Build the Scene

Start by designing the scene with character, setting, and emotional tension:

"Write a comedic scene where two rival coworkers are trapped in a supply closet and start passive-aggressively competing to seem the most 'chill' about it."

Then escalate:

"Now add a slowly leaking water pipe that starts dripping on one character, but they refuse to admit it's bothering them."

Then ask for punch-up:

"Give this scene a bigger visual payoff—something absurd but grounded that could turn this into a GIF-worthy moment."

Bringing in AI Visualization

Once your scene is written, you can use AI image generation tools to visualize key frames. This helps with:

- **Blocking** (Where are the characters? How do they move?)
- **Prop and costume gags** (What does the outfit say before a word is spoken?)
- **Set comedy** (What's in the background? What signage can add to the joke?)

Prompt ideas for image generation:

- "A character stuck halfway through a doggy door while still holding a briefcase."
- "Two roommates arguing in a kitchen filled with smoke, wearing wildly inappropriate outfits for the situation."
- "A passive-aggressive office birthday party where everyone is standing too far apart with forced smiles."

Use these images to:

- Pitch your show or scene with a visual hook.
- Storyboard your beats like a comic strip.
- Discover new gags just by seeing how weird a moment looks frozen in time.

Designing with Iconic Intent

You're not just visualizing to make things pretty. You're designing for impact. Ask:

- *If this scene had no dialogue, would it still be funny?*
- *If this moment became a meme or a poster, what would it say about the show?*
- *Is there something visually unexpected happening that makes this scene unique?*

Use ChatGPT to explore dialogue-free gags:

"Describe a visual comedy scene that could play out in silence but still make the audience laugh through character behavior alone."

Or:

"Write a slapstick-style physical scene between a high-strung chef and a clumsy intern in a narrow kitchen."

Combining Script and Image

When you merge script excerpts with AI-generated visuals, you create something powerful: a pitchable, storyboarded, pre-mapped comedy experience. This is great for:

- Selling your pilot
- Planning beats for shooting
- Building your writer's room visual language

Ask ChatGPT to generate a one-page pitch scene with visual notes like:

"Write a comedy scene between a parent and teen at the DMV. Include visual cues for blocking, reactions, and comedic props."

Then pair with an AI-generated image:

"Parent and teen at DMV counter, the teen slouched in a hoodie covered in ironic patches, the parent standing way too close to a visibly annoyed clerk. Fluorescent lights, line of bored people in background."

Final Tip: Funny Is in the Frame

Don't just write what's *said*. Write what's *seen*. If your scene doesn't work with the sound off, it's not iconic yet. If the camera can catch a joke before the actor speaks, you're golden. Visual comedy lives in silence, repetition, symmetry, awkwardness, and contradiction.

So whether it's a character carrying way too many balloons through a revolving door, or two people trying to eat spaghetti on a Zoom call while pretending not to hate each other—if you can *see* it before you *write* it, you're one step closer to creating a moment that audiences never forget.

Testing If a Joke Works with ChatGPT's Help

Every comedy writer knows the feeling: you've just written a line that *feels* funny—but is it really? Will it land with an audience, or does it just sound clever in your head at 1:00 a.m.? Comedy is notoriously hard to judge in isolation. That's why TV writers test material in a room. But if you're working solo—or trying to refine jokes before your writing partner's even had coffee—ChatGPT can become your instant feedback loop, comedy workshop, and punch-up partner.

In this chapter, we'll explore how to use ChatGPT to test jokes, tweak them, and even discover why a gag might be falling flat. It's not about handing over your comedy instincts—it's about using AI to sharpen them.

Step One: Test the Setup

Before a punchline can hit, the setup has to work. Start by showing ChatGPT your setup line and asking if it's clear, concise, and funny-ready.

Try this:

"Here's a setup for a joke: 'Karen bought a new meditation app just so she could yell at it.' Does this setup work? How could I make it tighter or more surprising?"

ChatGPT might suggest trimming it to:

"Karen downloaded a meditation app just to scream at the guided breathing."

That's already funnier—shorter, cleaner, and more character-specific. Even if you disagree, the process helps you *hear* the joke differently.

Step Two: Punchline Feedback

Sometimes your punchline feels flat, too obvious, or over-explained. Let ChatGPT help with structure and surprise.

Try:

"Setup: 'I asked my roommate to do the dishes.' Punchline: 'He said he's on a spiritual journey to avoid responsibility.' Does this work? Can you give me stronger variations?"

ChatGPT might return with:

- "He lit incense and said, 'I've released all attachment to clean plates.'"
- "He said he's dishwashing-adjacent—emotionally, not practically."
- "He bowed and whispered, 'I've ascended beyond soap.'"

This isn't about replacing your voice. It's about discovering *angles*—irony, rhythm, reversals, or idiom flips you hadn't considered.

Step Three: Misdirection and Surprise

One of the most effective tools in comedy is **misdirection**—leading the audience one way and veering off at the last second. You can ask ChatGPT to assess whether your line has enough twist.

Prompt:

"I'm trying to write a misdirect punchline. Setup: 'My therapist said I should sit with my emotions.' Current punchline: 'So now I cry on a beanbag chair.' Does this twist enough? Give me alternatives with more surprise."

ChatGPT might offer:

- "So I invited them all over for dinner and we haven't stopped arguing since."
- "Now my emotions and I split the rent."
- "So I gave them names and started a podcast."

See how each version uses the structure of the setup to twist toward something unexpected—*but logical within the emotional context*?

Step Four: Test for Tone and Audience

Comedy isn't universal—what's hilarious in one tone or genre might tank in another. Use ChatGPT to check tone fit.

Prompt:

"Here's a joke for a workplace sitcom: 'He keeps a stress ball on his desk, but it's filled with glitter and passive-aggression.' Does this fit a dry tone? Can you adjust it for a broader or more absurd show?"

Or test audience levels:

"Is this joke too niche? 'This salad is so dry, I'm getting Facebook Marketplace flashbacks.' Would general audiences get that?"

You can adjust from niche to broad by replacing references or adding context, without losing your style.

Step Five: Escalate or Trim

You've got a good joke—but can it be great? Ask ChatGPT to either build on it or streamline it.

Try:

"Punchline: 'He ghosted me, so I ghosted back. Now we're both haunting our mutuals.' Can you escalate this for a callback or running gag?"

Or:

"This joke feels overwritten. Can you trim it while keeping the punch?"

AI might help reshape it into:

- "Now we just send each other cryptic emoji at 2 a.m."

- "We're co-parenting the group chat in silent resentment."

Sometimes, less is more. Sometimes, more is funnier. ChatGPT can explore both without ego.

Step Six: Reformat for Delivery

A joke on paper isn't the same as one spoken out loud or delivered by a character. Ask ChatGPT to reshape your line to match a character's voice or delivery.

Prompt:

"Make this joke sound like it's coming from a deadpan introvert in their thirties."

Or

"Rewrite this line for a fast-talking character who overexplains everything."

This helps you not only refine the joke—but anchor it in character, where it will always be funniest.

Bonus: The Gut Check

When in doubt, run this classic test:

"Does this joke make sense on its own? Can it stand without setup context? Does it work visually, emotionally, or rhythmically?"

You can even try:

"Rate this joke on clarity, originality, and tone-fit. Suggest improvements if it scores low."

It's like a writers' room without needing coffee or scheduling six people.

Final Tip: You're Still the Comic Instinct

ChatGPT can't *feel* the joke land—but you can. Use it like a soundboard, a joke gym, a pitch wall. Don't expect it to hand you brilliance. Use it to *bounce your brilliance off of*, until it echoes back sharper.

Because sometimes all a joke needs is a second look, a shorter beat, or a better verb.

And sometimes? The joke is already perfect. But you didn't know that—until you heard it read back to you by a very polite robot.

Pulling Comedy from Real Life Experiences

The funniest stories often don't start in a writer's room—they happen at weddings, in waiting rooms, during awkward first dates, or while standing in line behind someone arguing with a vending machine. Real life is one giant, glorious mess of absurdity. And comedy thrives in the mess. Whether it's an embarrassing moment, a petty argument, a social faux pas, or a quiet emotional breakdown at a kid's birthday party—these moments *feel* funny because they *are* honest.

Writing comedy from real life doesn't mean copying exactly what happened. It means recognizing the emotional logic of that experience—what it felt like, why it spiraled, how you reacted—and then exaggerating it just enough to reveal the universal truth inside the personal chaos.

Start with the Emotional Core

Every great comedic moment has an emotional engine: insecurity, jealousy, fear, pride, neediness, shame, hope. That's where the comedy lives—not in the incident itself, but in how a person tries (and fails) to navigate it.

You don't have to tell the truth word-for-word. You just have to preserve the *emotional truth*. Ask yourself:

- What made the moment funny in hindsight?
- What was at stake for me, even if it seemed small?
- What did I believe about myself or the situation that turned out to be wrong?

Use ChatGPT to help you shape these:

"I once locked myself out of my car during a job interview. Can you turn this into a scene where the character tries to spin it as a personality strength?"

"Write a monologue based on someone trying to explain why they cried during a haircut."

Find the Exaggeration Point

Comedy often comes from turning up the dial *just a bit*. If you were nervous during a meeting, the character has a full-body sweat and drinks seven glasses of water. If you accidentally texted the wrong person, your character texts the *entire company*. The key is to blow it up just enough that it's funnier than real life—but still *plausible in emotion*.

Try this exercise:

Think of a moment in your life that made you cringe. Then ask ChatGPT:

"What's an exaggerated version of this story that still keeps the original feeling, but adds chaos?"

Maybe your real story is:

"I laughed during a serious work presentation because the font reminded me of a meme."

The comedy version becomes:

"They couldn't stop laughing and got asked to leave—only to discover they were the next presenter."

Characters Make It Funny

Sometimes the moment itself isn't hilarious until you add characters with specific flaws. You forgot your partner's birthday? That's awkward. But make the character an obsessive calendar-keeper who writes down *everything*, and now it's a character-based joke. They didn't just forget—they forgot *despite their own system.*

Let ChatGPT help you with:

"Rewrite this moment where someone ruins a surprise party—but make them a character who is obsessed with secrecy and always ruins it anyway."

Or:

"Write a scene where a perfectionist completely loses it because someone used the wrong type of spoon during a family dinner."

Embrace the Awkward

Audiences love awkward comedy because it's real. The long pause. The over-explanation. The attempt to backtrack that only makes things worse. If it was uncomfortable in the moment, it's probably gold now. What matters is *letting it breathe*—don't rush past the awkwardness. Lean into it.

Try:

"Write a dinner party scene inspired by the time I got someone's name wrong repeatedly—and only realized it when I saw it written on their birthday cake."

Or:

"Write a character monologue based on someone realizing their Zoom mic wasn't muted while they made sarcastic commentary the whole time."

The Power of Reframing

Sometimes your worst moment becomes your best material—once you stop trying to make yourself look good. Comedy doesn't reward perfection. It rewards honesty and collapse. So don't protect your ego in your writing. Let the character fall. Let them say the wrong thing. Let them break their own rules.

Reframe pain with ChatGPT like this:

"Turn this sad memory into a comic one: I showed up for a date on the wrong day and sat at the bar alone for an hour."

Or:

"I accidentally insulted someone's baby name thinking it was a joke. How would that look in a sitcom?"

Keep a Real-Life Joke Journal

To fuel your comedy writing, keep a running list of:

- Weird overheard conversations

- Moments that made you laugh despite yourself
- Social situations that spiraled
- Accidental lies you told
- Things you regret—but find strangely hilarious now

Bring these moments to ChatGPT:

"I once panicked at airport security and said I had 'nothing illegal *today*.' Turn this into a sitcom beat."

Or:

"At a wedding, I got mistaken for the caterer and just went with it. Can you create a running gag from that?"

Final Thought: It's Funny Because It's True (But Not Boring)

Real-life comedy isn't about copying life—it's about *mining it*. When your audience recognizes the moment—not necessarily the plot, but the *feeling*—they connect. They laugh not because it's outrageous, but because it's real... and thank God it's not happening to *them*.

So tell the story. Embellish it. Twist it. Break it open. And laugh at yourself on the page, so your audience can laugh with you.

Writing Comedic Flashbacks, Fantasies, and Dream Sequences

Comedy doesn't have to follow the rules of time and space. In fact, some of the best laughs happen when you break reality entirely—just for a moment. Flashbacks, fantasies, and dream sequences are comedic gold mines. They let your characters relive their worst moments, imagine their best lives, or spiral into ridiculous mental tangents. These moments are fast, weird, stylized—and unforgettable. When used right, they deepen character, heighten absurdity, and keep your audience guessing what's real and what's hilariously not.

So how do you write them?

Why These Sequences Work in Comedy

Flashbacks show who your character used to be—or who they *still are* under the surface.

Fantasies show what your character wants—or fears.

Dream sequences show how chaotic their inner world really is.

They're tools for contradiction. A character says they were calm in an emergency... cut to them screaming and breaking a window. They say they don't care about someone... cut to them imagining a wedding. These scenes break structure to reveal truth—and the more absurd the execution, the harder they land.

Flashbacks: Comic Lies Exposed

The best flashbacks undercut what your character just said. It's about the difference between *what they claim* and *what actually happened*. This is perfect for characters who lie, exaggerate, or live in denial.

Example:

Character: "I handled the breakup like a total adult."

Flashback: They're hiding in a bush outside their ex's apartment eating chocolate with binoculars.

You can use ChatGPT to workshop:

"Write a flashback that contradicts a character's memory of being heroic during a camping trip."

Or

"Give me three comedic flashbacks to a character's failed attempts to act cool at high school dances."

Flashbacks also work as **running gags**—each one escalating. Every time the character says "I learned my lesson," we see yet another version of them failing to learn it.

Fantasies: Wanting Too Much, Too Specifically

Comedic fantasy sequences are usually over-the-top, painfully earnest, or deliciously petty. They show us what a character thinks they deserve—or *wishes* would happen. Fantasies are especially funny when contrasted with reality.

Example:

Character imagines storming into a meeting, commanding respect, and getting applause.

Cut to: They walk into the room and immediately trip on a chair.

Fantasies are great for:

- Visual jokes (slow motion, music, lighting)
- Character desires (romantic, professional, egotistical)
- Comic reveals (we don't realize it's a fantasy until it ends)

Try this with ChatGPT:

"Write a fantasy where a shy character imagines giving the perfect comeback speech, but it turns into a musical number."

Or

"A character envisions their enemy being humiliated at a wedding—but it backfires."

Fantasies can also play with **genre**. Maybe the character's fantasy is filmed like a spy movie, a noir detective monologue, or a nature documentary narrated by David Attenborough. The bigger the contrast, the funnier the moment.

Dream Sequences: Chaos with Purpose

Dreams are where logic fully breaks—and that makes them incredible playgrounds for surreal humor. But even chaos needs an emotional spine. A dream sequence should *reflect* what the character is struggling with—just through strange symbols, exaggerated fears, or visual nonsense.

Example:

A character afraid of being replaced dreams they're literally turned into a potted plant and everyone treats it as normal.

Dreams are great when:

- Characters speak out of character.
- Normal rules don't apply (physics, identity, time).
- The visuals are bold and strange.
- The comedy comes from logic being *almost* right.

Use ChatGPT to explore:

"Write a dream sequence where a character's imposter syndrome turns into a courtroom trial with talking furniture."

Or

"A dream where everyone speaks in compliments but the character hears only insults."

Dreams are also good places for visual callbacks—props, people, or phrases from earlier episodes showing up in twisted or hilarious ways. That's what makes the sequence feel earned rather than random.

Formatting and Pacing Tips

- **Make it short.** These sequences should punch in, hit hard, and punch out. The longer they run, the harder it is to keep the momentum.
- **Use bold transitions.** In your script, label these sequences clearly:
    - *FLASHBACK – INT. DANCE FLOOR – NIGHT (2009)*
    - *FANTASY – INT. WHITE HOUSE – DAY (IN HER HEAD)*
    - *DREAM SEQUENCE – INT. GIANT CHEESE MAZE – UNKNOWN TIME*
- **Keep dialogue stylized.** People talk differently in dreams and fantasies—let the lines be exaggerated, poetic, robotic, or weirdly perfect.
- **Visual gags are king.** These are your moments to show a character's inner mess or ego *without* needing exposition. Think sight gags, slow zooms, wild costumes, impossible staging.

When to Use Them

Don't throw in a dream or fantasy just for novelty. Ask:

- *Is this showing us something the character can't say out loud?*
- *Does it reveal a fear, need, or delusion?*
- *Does it punch up the joke or the truth?*

These sequences work best when they contrast reality. When the fantasy cuts back to real life—and the character is still standing in the hallway holding a bucket of salad—that's when the audience laughs the loudest.

Final Tip: Let the Absurdity Serve the Honesty

The most memorable comedic fantasies and flashbacks don't just go big—they go *real.* Not in plot, but in emotion. What's funny isn't just that the character dreamed they were the Queen of England—it's that they believed that was the only way to finally be heard.

When to Break the Fourth Wall (and When Not To)

Breaking the fourth wall is one of comedy's flashiest tools. When used well, it creates intimacy, surprise, and brilliant self-awareness. The audience feels like they're in on the joke. The character becomes more than a player in the story—they become the storyteller, the confessor, the unreliable narrator with a wink. But when used poorly, breaking the fourth wall can feel like a gimmick. It can kill pacing, ruin immersion, or scream, "Look how clever I am!" without actually being clever.

So how do you know when to break the fourth wall—and more importantly, when not to?

What It Actually Means

The "fourth wall" is the imaginary barrier between the characters and the audience. Most of the time, that wall is invisible but firmly in place. When a character turns and speaks directly to the viewer, they're breaking that wall—acknowledging that they know they're in a story, or letting us know that *we* know they're in on something bigger.

Famous examples include:

- *Fleabag*, where the main character uses fourth-wall breaks for confessions, commentary, and emotional shifts.
- *Deadpool*, where the breaks are brash, meta, and relentlessly self-referential.
- *The Office* and *Modern Family*, which use documentary-style looks-to-camera that double as silent commentary or non-verbal punchlines.

Each of these uses the technique for different reasons. So let's break it down.

When to Break the Fourth Wall

1. To Build a Relationship with the Audience

In *Fleabag*, the fourth wall break is more than a joke device—it's a lifeline. The character lets us into her head. The wry smirks, whispered asides, and mid-scene commentary create an emotional intimacy. The audience becomes her closest companion—until, of course, that closeness gets challenged.

Use it like this:

- When your character has no one else they can be honest with.
- When their public and private selves are wildly different.
- When the audience's insight makes the moment funnier, sadder, or more complex.

Try ChatGPT to develop this:

"Write a scene where a character breaks the fourth wall to confess something they can't say to anyone else—but still try to keep their cool while doing it."

2. For Irony, Commentary, or Satire

If your show is meta, self-aware, or mocking genre tropes, a fourth-wall break can be an amazing comedic weapon. Think of it as the character pressing pause to call out the formula, hypocrisy, or absurdity of the moment.

Examples:

- "If this were a romantic comedy, this is where I'd say something vulnerable. But I'm a Capricorn, so... pass."
- "Yes, I know. We're doing the 'unexpected baby reveal' thing now. I don't like it either."

Use it when:

- The show is making fun of itself, TV tropes, or societal expectations.
- You want to highlight a contradiction the characters *won't* say out loud.

Ask ChatGPT:

"Write a fourth-wall break where a character acknowledges that they're stuck in a cliché scene and try to rewrite it on the spot."

3. For Punchlines and Pacing

Sometimes, a quick look to the camera is the entire joke. A dry expression. A raised eyebrow. A blink after someone says something absurd. You don't need a monologue—just a connection. In documentary-style comedies like *The Office* or *Parks and Rec*, this silent exchange *is* the rhythm. It replaces a punchline with a *reaction.*

Use it when:

- A character hears something outrageous and the audience needs to *feel* their unspoken response.
- The comedy lives in the awkward silence between what was said and what was felt.

When Not to Break the Fourth Wall

1. When It Undermines the Scene's Emotion

If your characters are in a truly vulnerable, grounded moment, breaking the fourth wall can kill the emotion. It reminds the audience it's all a show—which is the last thing you want when something *real* is finally happening.

Don't do it:

- In the middle of a death, breakup, or reveal that depends on full immersion.
- If your character is being fully authentic with another person on-screen. They don't need *us* in that moment.

2. When It Becomes a Crutch

If your character is always turning to the audience instead of dealing with people in the scene, the fourth-wall break can become a form of avoidance. The stakes get lower. The show starts to feel like a monologue instead of a story.

Ask yourself:

- Is this moment better served by an awkward silence or interaction?
- Is the audience the right person to hear this thought—or should the character be forced to *say it out loud* to someone in the room?

3. When It Doesn't Fit the World You Built

Not every show can support a fourth-wall break. In a grounded family comedy, it might feel out of place. In a high-concept farce, it might feel *too* normal. You want the fourth wall to feel like it belongs to the tone and rhythm of the world you've created.

Ask ChatGPT to test the tone:

"Does this fourth-wall break make sense in a grounded workplace comedy—or should it be delivered through dialogue instead?"

How to Use It Effectively

- **Set a rule.** Can *only one character* break the wall? Is it internal or shared across characters?
- **Use it sparingly.** The first time it happens, it's novel. The second time, it's style. The fifteenth? It better be *building* something.
- **Let it evolve.** In *Fleabag*, the audience starts as a safety net. Then it becomes a problem. Your use of the technique should shift with the character's journey.

Final Thought

Breaking the fourth wall works best when it's not just clever—but *necessary*. When it reveals something no one else can. When it makes the audience lean in instead of pulling away. When it feels like a secret shared, not a spotlight turned.

So yes—wink at us. Whisper to us. Roll your eyes with us. But only if you've earned it.

Casting Your Characters in Your Mind (or on the Page)

Before the first joke lands, before the first table read, even before you finish the script—comedy lives and dies by who says what. Not just the *lines*, but the *voices* behind them. The rhythm, the energy, the facial expressions you picture as you write. That's why "casting in your mind" is a powerful creative tool—because once you know who your characters *are*, you can write for them like they're real people. You can hear their delivery, their timing, their contradictions. And if you're lucky, the audience will too.

Even if your show never makes it to production, casting your characters on the page helps you:

- Write clearer dialogue.
- Define energy levels between characters.
- Avoid "same voice syndrome" where everyone sounds alike.
- Make each scene feel alive and performable.

So how do you cast your comedy effectively—whether in your imagination or your script?

Start with Type, Not Tropes

Avoid cardboard archetypes like "the funny one" or "the hot mess." Instead, think in terms of emotional drives and comic contradictions. Great comedic characters are walking paradoxes:

- The life coach who cries during inspirational speeches.
- The chill guy who's wildly controlling about recycling.
- The confident disaster who talks in motivational quotes but panics at feedback.

Ask ChatGPT:

"Give me character descriptions for five comedic personalities, each with a contradiction at the core."

Or

"Create a character who thinks they're the voice of reason but is secretly the biggest instigator."

You're not looking for caricatures—you're looking for internal *pressure*. That's what makes a line funny before it's even spoken.

Cast Real People in Your Head (Even If You Never Say Their Names)

Think of comedians, actors, or people you know who could *live* in that role. Maybe your character talks like Maya Rudolph but moves like Rowan Atkinson. Maybe they have the insecure confidence of a young Jonah Hill and the fashion choices of a high school principal on vacation.

Use casting types to anchor tone:

- Is this a dry, deadpan role? (Think Aubrey Plaza, Jemaine Clement, or Steven Wright.)
- Is this a high-energy chaos machine? (Think Melissa McCarthy, Chris Farley, or Tiffany Haddish.)
- Is this the straight man with hidden depth? (Think John Krasinski, Rashida Jones, or Jason Bateman.)

Even if you're not naming these actors in your script, picturing them as you write helps you build comic rhythm and reaction.

Ask ChatGPT:

"Suggest five modern actor types who could play a fast-talking, insecure assistant with delusions of grandeur."

Or

"I want a warm, lovable oddball who's surprisingly profound—who are some casting inspirations for that energy?"

Write Physical Comedy into the Personality

When you picture your cast, don't just hear their voice—*see* how they move. Physicality is part of the character. Are they big and expressive? Small and twitchy? Do they gesture too much or not at all? Are they constantly adjusting their clothes, hair, or environment?

Use this in your descriptions:

"She walks like she's apologizing to gravity."

"He sits like his body was poured into the chair in a hurry."

"They never stop pacing unless someone says their name."

These details build comedy without dialogue—and give actors something to work with, even if the actor only exists in your imagination.

Balance Your Cast Dynamically

Every great comedy ensemble works because the characters contrast and complement each other. Think *The Office*, *Parks and Rec*, *Arrested Development*, or *Schitt's Creek*. They all feature:

- The grounded realist (or supposed realist)
- The chaos engine
- The delusional dreamer
- The anxious skeptic
- The wildcard who surprises everyone (including themselves)

Ask ChatGPT:

"Build a five-character comedic ensemble where each personality creates conflict and contrast with the others."

Or

"Create character pairings that naturally generate comedy through tension and misunderstanding."

Use archetype contrast to design scenes where no two characters respond the same way to a situation. That's where comedy lives—in *difference*, not sameness.

Audition Your Dialogue

Once you've mentally cast your roles, test your dialogue out loud. Does the line sound like that person? Or like a generic comedy quip? You can even assign voices to ChatGPT:

"Rewrite this dialogue with Character A sounding like Kristen Wiig's awkward energy and Character B sounding like Hannibal Buress's dry sarcasm."

Or:

"Run a comedic dialogue scene between a hyperactive optimist and a burnt-out realist reacting to a surprise baby shower."

This helps lock in tone, rhythm, and delivery—before you ever reach a stage.

Optional: Casting on the Page (Without Saying It)

If you're pitching your show, you might reference a casting "type" in the show bible or character breakdown. You're not saying, "This is for Bill Hader"—you're saying, "Think Bill Hader meets Daniel Radcliffe's weirdness in *Miracle Workers*." It's a shortcut for tone and delivery.

Example:

KEIRA (30s) – She's your hyper-competent friend who could run a company or a cult. Think Catherine O'Hara energy in *Schitt's Creek* with the self-importance of a Gwyneth Paltrow lifestyle blog.

Or:

RAYMOND (50s) – Picture a retired magician turned HR manager. Dry, mystical, full of tragic optimism. Somewhere between *David Brent* and *The Dude*, but more buttoned-up.

Casting your characters in your mind—or directly on the page—isn't about stunt-casting or fantasy football. It's about clarity. About shaping voices that are distinct, alive, and full of comic tension. Once you know *who's* in the scene, the jokes write themselves. Not because you're trying harder, but because the character is already doing the work. So cast boldly. Be specific. Picture the smirk, the pause, the hand wave, the stumble. Write like that actor *already lives* in your story. And the audience? They'll hear the voice before the credits even roll.

Making Every Line Count in a 22-Minute Episode

A 22-minute comedy episode is like a tightly packed suitcase—there's no room for fluff, and every item you cram in better serve a purpose. With only around 30 pages of script to work with, each line must carry weight. Every bit of dialogue, every glance, every joke, every silence—it all has to serve the story, the character, the rhythm, or the laugh. There's no time for characters to meander, no space for scenes that don't push forward, and certainly no luxury for lines that just sit there looking clever.

If you want your episode to be punchy, sharp, and deeply rewatchable, you've got to treat every line like it's fighting for its life.

Start with Purpose: What Is This Line Doing?

Before a line earns a spot in your script, ask:

- Does it advance the plot?
- Does it reveal character?
- Does it build or break tension?
- Is it funny?
- Is it a setup or payoff?
- Does it contrast or escalate?

If the answer is "not really" or "kinda," cut or rewrite it. Lean into lines that multitask—those are the ones that sing.

Try this with ChatGPT:

"Here's a line: 'You always do this.' Rewrite it so it reflects the speaker's fear of abandonment, sets up a later gag, and still sounds like something they'd say."

You'll find that with the right angle, a single line can reveal an emotional truth, land a joke, and set up the next beat.

Cut to the Joke (or the Emotion)

Comedy thrives on rhythm. If your line meanders to the punchline, you've lost it. Tighten it. Simplify it. Strip it to the core.

Example:

Long version: "I mean, it's kind of wild that you didn't tell me, considering everything we've been through. Don't you think?"

Tight version: "You ghosted me through a group trauma."

The shorter version hits harder, funnier, and faster. In a 22-minute script, you need *that* kind of momentum.

Ask ChatGPT:

"Punch up this paragraph into one sharp, funny line that keeps the same meaning."

Build Dialogue That Layers Meaning

In a strong episode, the best lines do more than talk—they echo. They return later with new context. They connect to the theme or episode title. They become running gags or the emotional spine. This kind of layered writing turns simple dialogue into storytelling shorthand.

For example:

- Early: "I don't believe in signs."
- Mid-episode: Character narrowly avoids a falling piano.
- Final line: "Okay, *maybe* that was a sign."

Let ChatGPT help you layer:

"Write a phrase that can work as a joke early in the episode and a callback with emotional weight at the end."

Silence Is a Line Too

Not every reaction needs dialogue. A look. A pause. A failed attempt to speak. A beat of silence after someone says something absurd—*that's part of the comedy*. In a 22-minute episode, using silence wisely adds texture and rhythm. It also gives the audience space to laugh, breathe, or lean in.

Use this technique especially:

- Right before or after punchlines
- During awkward moments
- To underscore emotional shifts

Try this:

"I have a scene where one character confesses something embarrassing. Help me rewrite it with more physical beats and fewer words, but keep it funny."

Structure Every Scene like a Mini Sketch

Each scene in a 22-minute comedy should feel like its own mini-play: setup, escalation, climax, punch-out. Don't let scenes wander. Get in late and leave early. Keep transitions tight. If the scene doesn't push the story forward or offer a great moment—cut it.

Use ChatGPT to test structure:

"Outline this three-page scene into setup, conflict, and punchline. Trim the fat."

Or:

"Rewrite this dialogue so it starts in the middle of the argument instead of building slowly."

Keep Character Voices Distinct

When time is short, you can't afford interchangeable dialogue. Each line should sound like *that character*—not just "someone funny." Their vocabulary, rhythm, insecurity, or swagger should shape every word.

Try this test:

"Give each of these three characters a one-line reaction to hearing they've been invited to a dinner party. Make sure their personalities are clear without explaining them."

This also helps you spot whose lines are doing the heavy lifting—and whose aren't pulling weight.

Use Line Economy to Pack in Jokes

One-liners are gold in short formats. But don't just jam in zingers—write lines that feel *inevitable*. The best jokes often come from:

- Contrast: "You brought soup to a knife fight?"
- Reversal: "That wasn't an apology. That was a Yelp review."
- Escalation: "We're not mad. We're just disappointed. In triplicate. With graphs."

Let ChatGPT give options:

"Rewrite this punchline in three ways: sarcastic, dry, and over-the-top sincere."

And use alt lines for variety:

"Give me five alt versions of this line that keep the tone but offer different punch styles."

Trim on the Rewrite Pass

On your second draft, cut 10% of your dialogue. You'll be amazed how many lines explain what's already clear. Instead of repeating, trust subtext, body language, or contrast with the next beat. Tighter lines = tighter episodes = tighter laughs.

Try:

"Here's a dialogue scene. Edit it for pacing, clarity, and punch. Keep the character voices."

Final Thought

A 22-minute comedy is a sprint. Every line is a step that has to carry weight, land clean, and move you forward. When you write with precision, character clarity, and rhythmic punch, even a five-word sentence can deepen a character, deliver a laugh, and become iconic.

So ask more from every line. Ask it to reveal, twist, echo, or surprise. If it doesn't—it doesn't belong.

Writing Comedy without a Writers' Room—Using AI as Your Team

Writing comedy alone can be exhilarating... until it's not. You hit a wall. You doubt the joke. You try three different punchlines and start to hate all of them. That's where a traditional writers' room would save the day—bantering, riffing, pitching alts, punching up lines until the scene sparkles. But what if you're flying solo? What if there's *no* room... just you, your ideas, and your blinking cursor?

Good news: You're not actually alone. With AI, especially ChatGPT, you can simulate the energy, rhythm, and chaotic brilliance of a real writers' room. You can bounce ideas, test jokes, pitch alternates, shape character arcs, and polish scenes—*all with a virtual team that never sleeps, interrupts, or needs coffee.*

Let's explore how to turn AI into your personal comedy writing crew.

1. Use AI as Your "Pitch Guy"

Every writers' room needs that person who throws 10 ideas at the wall so someone else can grab the best one. ChatGPT thrives in this role. You can rapid-fire prompts and get back a whole slate of setups, punchlines, or scene ideas in seconds.

Try:

"Give me 10 comedy episode premises for a roommate who thinks they're being spied on by their toaster."

Or

"Pitch five character-based jokes about someone trying to return a parrot to PetSmart."

Don't use everything—just see what sticks. Even bad ideas can spark good ones. That's how writers' rooms work.

2. Treat AI as Your Punch-Up Partner

Got a joke that's *almost* working? Let ChatGPT help punch it up. You don't need it to be perfect—you need variation, rhythm, perspective.

Prompt:

"Here's a line: 'You should see the other guy.' He's clearly lying. Give me five punch-up versions that are funnier, darker, or weirder."

Or:

"She's trying to sound smart but keeps misusing words. Rewrite this speech with malapropisms that still sound believable."

You can even assign comedic tone:

"Make this line sharper, but keep it in a dry, deadpan style."

3. Use AI to Test Scene Dynamics

Working alone means you don't always notice when scenes sag. Use ChatGPT to evaluate a scene's shape.

Prompt:

"Here's a three-page scene. Does it escalate? Are the character motivations clear? Is the pacing right? Suggest trims or tweaks."

Or better yet:

"Rewrite this dialogue as a more comedic escalation. Keep the conflict the same, but build to a bigger payoff."

Suddenly, you're not editing in a vacuum—you're getting notes that help sharpen rhythm and tension.

4. Create a Mock Writers' Room on Demand

Want a room full of voices? Simulate one.

Prompt:

"Act as three comedy writers: one is absurd, one is sarcastic, one is grounded. I'll pitch a scene, and I want you to each respond with your take."

Now you have *conflicting perspectives*—which is exactly what you'd get in a real writers' room. And like in a real room, *tension creates clarity.*

You can prompt them to argue:

"Let the sarcastic writer hate the absurd pitch and try to fix it. Let the grounded one suggest a new setup that makes it more realistic."

You've got your chaos. Now find your clarity.

5. Use AI to Build and Maintain a Show Bible

Writers' rooms are built on shared memory—who a character is, what happened last season, what gags are running. You can use ChatGPT to track your series logic.

Try:

"Summarize everything we know about this character so far: personality, voice, biggest moments, contradictions."

Or

"Build me a one-page show bible with character descriptions, tone, setting, and five episode synopses."

This isn't just for pitching—it helps *you* stay consistent across episodes, scenes, and jokes.

6. Workshop Dialogue like a Table Read

Have ChatGPT read your scene like actors around the table.

Prompt:

"Play this scene out with characters A, B, and C. Read it like a table read. Emphasize tone, delivery, and rhythm."

You'll start hearing things differently—lines that drag, jokes that could land sharper, beats that need a pause.

You can follow up with:

"Give me alternate line reads for this joke: one smug, one panicked, one dead serious."

Suddenly, you're not just hearing text—you're hearing performance.

7. Keep a Digital Comedy Wall

In a real writers' room, there's a whiteboard or corkboard where jokes, ideas, bits, and titles live. You can simulate that by using ChatGPT to collect and organize running gags, alt lines, or scene starters.

Prompt:

"Create a running gag list for a comedy series about two incompetent bounty hunters."

Or

"Make a chart of ten funny cold opens, five episode arcs, and recurring side characters with strong comic voices."

It becomes your digital idea bank—a place to return to when you hit a wall.

8. Don't Forget to Argue With It

AI doesn't have an ego—but *you* should. If a joke doesn't feel right, push back.

Try:

"That rewrite feels too soft. Make it edgier, but keep the emotional truth intact."

Or

"This joke works logically, but not emotionally. Pitch three versions that lean into character flaws."

You're not just taking suggestions—you're *refining your own voice* through creative debate.

Final Thought: You're Still the Head Writer

AI can act like a room, a reader, a rewriter, even a heckler. But *you're* the showrunner. The taste. The final call. Comedy is personal—it's your weird voice, your take on relationships, failure, awkwardness, ego, identity, and everything in between. The point of using AI isn't to give up control—it's to give yourself momentum. To simulate the chatter, friction, and flow of a comedy brain trust—even when it's just you and your laptop.

So if you're writing alone, you're not *really* alone. You've got a room on standby. You've got a writing partner who never runs out of energy. And you've got a way to keep the ideas coming—even when your coffee runs out.

Developing a Series That Can Evolve and Stay Funny

Every great comedy series starts funny—but the ones we remember? They *stay* funny, even as the world around them, and the characters within them, change. Longevity in comedy doesn't come from recycling punchlines or keeping characters frozen in time. It comes from building a world flexible enough to grow, characters flawed enough to change (or try to), and comedic engines strong enough to adapt to new situations. If your series can evolve without losing its soul, you won't just have a funny show—you'll have one people come back to year after year.

So how do you design a comedy series with staying power?

1. Start with a Flexible Premise, Not a Gimmick

A strong premise gives you comedy fuel for multiple seasons. A *gimmick* might get you laughs in the pilot—but it traps you fast. Think about shows like *The Office*, *Brooklyn Nine-Nine*, or *Parks and Rec*. All of them start with a clear, structured environment (workplace, precinct, government office), but the comedy comes from the people in it—not just the setup.

Your premise should answer:

- Can this world sustain new problems and characters?
- Are there rules and roles that create natural tension?
- Is this a situation where people will constantly want different things?

Try ChatGPT:

"Pitch five comedy series ideas where the premise allows for ongoing tension, growth, and rotating stories."

Or

"Help me rework this single-situation comedy so it can expand beyond its first season."

2. Create Characters Who Can Change Just Enough

Audiences love familiarity—but they crave growth. Your characters shouldn't evolve overnight, but they *should* change in small, funny, often reluctant ways. Give each of them a contradiction: something they *think* they are, and something they're actually afraid of being. That gap is where both the comedy and the arc live.

Examples:

- A self-declared alpha who secretly wants to be liked.
- A cynic who keeps accidentally falling in love with things.
- A peacekeeper who eventually snaps in the most dramatic way.

Ask ChatGPT:

"Create five character arcs for a comedy ensemble that let each character grow or fail to grow in funny, surprising ways."

Remember: change doesn't always mean growth. Regressing, relapsing, or shifting sideways is often funnier—and more human—than improving.

3. Build Running Gags That Can Evolve

Recurring jokes give your show rhythm and identity. But to stay funny, they need to *change shape*. A catchphrase can grow into a moment of emotional vulnerability. A throwaway line in season one can become a key character trait in season three.

Running gags that evolve:

- A character known for outrageous lies becomes the only one telling the truth—no one believes them.
- An ongoing bit about failed inventions becomes a startup subplot.
- A fake relationship joke turns real and creates chaos.

Use ChatGPT:

"Take this running gag and show how it could evolve emotionally or dramatically over several seasons."

Or

"Create five running jokes that begin as character quirks and grow into story arcs."

4. Let the Relationships Drive the Show

If plot is the body, relationships are the heartbeat. The best comedies don't just throw characters into new situations—they let dynamics *change* over time.

Examples:

- Rivals becoming friends (reluctantly).
- A will-they-won't-they that turns into a bad relationship... and then a weird friendship.
- A mentor who slowly realizes the mentee is surpassing them.

Try this:

"Design a five-season friendship arc between two mismatched characters who start off hating each other."

Or

"Create episodic stories that deepen a codependent relationship without making it too sentimental."

When relationships evolve, the comedy deepens. The laughs aren't just from jokes—they're from history.

5. Add New Characters without Breaking the Tone

New blood can refresh a show—but only if it fits the existing comic DNA. Bring in characters who:

- Challenge the group dynamic.
- Reflect how far the original characters have come (or haven't).

- Introduce new comic energy without replacing core identities.

Test character additions with ChatGPT:

"Pitch a new character for season 3 who threatens the main duo's dynamic but brings fresh energy."

Or

"Suggest new side characters that can spin off subplots without stealing focus."

The goal is expansion, not replacement.

6. Change Settings without Changing the Soul

A great show can change locations, careers, or situations—as long as it keeps its emotional core. A high school comedy can become a college one. A workplace comedy can shift to a startup. The key is making sure the *stakes and conflicts* still reflect the character flaws and desires that powered the early episodes.

Try:

"If this series moved from a small town to a big city, how would the characters stay funny and true to themselves?"

Or:

"Suggest ways to evolve a comedy setting across five seasons that reflects deeper character arcs."

7. Track the Tone—but Let It Mature

Early episodes might lean heavily on gags and quirk. As your show grows, you can earn emotional beats—without sacrificing humor. Think *BoJack Horseman*, *Fleabag*, or *Ted Lasso*. Let your characters get more layered. Let the jokes get sharper or weirder. Let the emotional moments land harder because the audience now *knows* these people.

Ask ChatGPT:

"How can I mature the tone of a silly workplace comedy by season three without losing laughs?"

Or

"Give me examples of episodes that deepen emotional themes while still delivering hard comedy."

The funniest shows don't stay funny by staying the same. They evolve. Not in spite of their structure, but *because of it*. They grow their world, their characters, and their emotional stakes without ever abandoning their tone. They surprise the audience with moments of truth—then hit them with a joke so perfect it could only come *right then*. So as you write your series, think beyond episode one. Think season arcs, relationship shifts, long-game setups. Let your show have room to breathe, stumble, and get back up—because if it can evolve while still making people laugh, it won't just be a show.

It'll be *a classic*.

Using Callback Humor over a Whole Season

One of the most satisfying feelings in comedy is when a joke returns—bigger, funnier, and sharper than before. That's the power of callback humor. It rewards your audience for paying attention. It creates inside jokes between the show and the viewer. And when used across an entire season, callback humor can build a rhythm that ties episodes together, gives your characters depth, and transforms a small moment into a full-circle payoff.

Callback humor isn't just a funny repeat. It's an echo, a remix, a narrative boomerang. Done well, it gives your show a signature feel—where the laughs don't just come from what's new, but from how well you've woven the old into it.

What Is a Callback, Really?

At its simplest, a callback is a reference to an earlier joke, line, event, or moment that returns later in the story. But not all callbacks are created equal. The strongest ones:

- Add new meaning to the original joke.
- Escalate or subvert what came before.
- Reward emotional or thematic investment—not just attention to detail.

They create a comedic "memory"—a pattern the audience recognizes and takes delight in.

Types of Callbacks Over a Season

1. The Running Gag

This is the most visible form of callback. A specific line, action, or quirk keeps appearing with variations. It can get bigger, more ridiculous, or ironically subtler as the season goes on.

Examples:

- A character who insists they've "got a guy" for everything... but the guy is always wildly inappropriate.
- Someone always invents new terms for ordinary things, like calling coffee "bean broth" or pizza "flat round joy."

ChatGPT can help you build these:

"Create a running gag for a character who misunderstands technology, escalating in each episode."

2. The Emotional Callback

This is where humor deepens connection. A joke that started as silly reappears at a key moment—but with emotional weight. It's funny because it matters *more* now.

Examples:

- A couple's first flirty exchange becomes their breakup line... and their reconciliation phrase.
- A line that once mocked someone becomes a moment of unexpected support when someone else uses it sincerely.

Use ChatGPT for shaping tone:

"Give me an emotional callback for a character who started the season as a loner but ends with a found family."

3. The Thematic Callback

This callback returns to an idea, fear, or habit—often highlighting character growth or stagnation. It may not be laugh-out-loud funny, but it's layered.

Examples:

- A character always says, "I don't do apologies"—but finally does, and it's a disaster.
- Someone who was obsessed with money early on later gives away something valuable... then makes a dry comment about how they'll invoice for the emotional labor.

ChatGPT prompt:

"Suggest five thematic callbacks that show a character slowly changing over a season, but still funny."

4. The Situational Callback

An entire scenario is repeated with new context. It's the same setup... but everyone reacts differently because of what they've been through.

Examples:

- In Episode 2, the team plans a surprise party that goes terribly. In Episode 10, they try again—worse. Or better. But different.
- The boss gives an identical motivational speech in Episodes 1, 6, and 12—each time met with a totally different response from the team.

Ask:

"How can I repeat a comic scene in a season finale to reflect how the characters have changed?"

How to Set Up a Callback that Lasts

Be Specific Early On

A callback can't work if the original moment was forgettable. Make the initial moment distinctive—a weird phrase, a visual oddity, a line with odd rhythm, a surprising contradiction. You're planting a seed.

Example:

Character insists on always wearing a "lucky" fanny pack. Everyone hates it. In the finale, the fanny pack saves the day—and nobody ever mentions it again.

Don't Overuse It

A callback needs space to breathe. If it shows up in every episode, it becomes predictable. Think of it like seasoning—not the main ingredient.

Ask ChatGPT:

"Take this one-liner and map three versions of how it could be used across a season: first as a joke, second as a theme, third as a twist."

Let It Grow

When you return to a joke, build on it. Let the delivery change. Let the context shift. Let the character's attitude about it evolve. The best callbacks aren't identical—they're *bigger*, *wiser*, or *messier* than the first time.

Example:

Episode 1: "I don't run unless I'm being chased."

Episode 6: The character *is* being chased—and they're walking.

Episode 10: They're jogging voluntarily—and hate every second of it.

Layering Callbacks across the Season

To make callbacks feel like part of your show's DNA:

- **Track your jokes**: Keep a list of phrases, bits, and beats worth revisiting.
- **Plan some and discover others**: Some callbacks you'll seed early. Others will surprise you in the rewrite.
- **Use different characters**: When a joke shifts from one character to another, it gains new power and play.

You can use ChatGPT to track and design:

"Help me build a callback tracker for a 10-episode comedy season, with places to escalate or subvert earlier jokes."

Final Thought

Callback humor is how you make your comedy feel bigger than the moment. It's how your series earns re-watch value. It's how a dumb line from Episode 3 becomes a legendary moment in Episode 10—not because the line changed, but because *we did*.

So write with memory. Plant the seed. Water it slowly. Then let it bloom in a way that catches everyone by surprise—while making them feel like they were in on the joke the whole time.

Creating a Comedy Show That Can Last More Than One Season

If writing a great comedy pilot is like delivering a perfect one-liner, then creating a show that lasts multiple seasons is like sustaining a killer set—building tension, timing your callbacks, letting your characters evolve, and always keeping the audience wanting more. A single-season comedy can be sharp and self-contained. But a multi-season series? That's a world. That's a place viewers want to live in, revisit, and quote at dinner parties for years to come.

So how do you design a comedy show with long-term potential? The kind that grows deeper, not just longer? The kind that feels fresh in Season Four instead of formulaic halfway through Season Two?

Let's break it down.

1. Build a World, Not Just a Premise

Your pilot might start with a simple "what if"—but to keep going, your world needs complexity, community, and flexibility. Whether it's an office, a family, a town, a support group, or a Dungeons & Dragons campaign, your setting should naturally generate conflict, change, and story without exhausting itself.

Ask yourself:

- Can this world realistically produce new problems every week?
- Is there a reason these characters are *stuck* together for the long haul?
- Can new characters enter without breaking the show?

If the answer's yes, you've got a world. If not, use ChatGPT to expand it:

"Help me build out a comedy series set in a laundromat, with secondary characters, evolving conflicts, and episode ideas beyond Season 1."

2. Design Evolving Character Arcs, Not Just Quirks

Characters make the show last. Not because they change radically—but because they *try to*. Audiences don't need happy endings; they need attempts. Your characters should have contradictions, blind spots, patterns they repeat, and moments of surprising clarity.

Create arcs with:

- Growth that's slow, funny, and reluctant.
- Failures that repeat... but escalate.
- Relationships that shift over time.

Try:

"Create a three-season arc for a character who thinks they're the 'glue' of the group but is actually the source of most problems."

This keeps the comedy personal and prevents stagnation.

3. Layer In Long-Term Mysteries or Themes

Plot twists aren't just for dramas. A well-seeded mystery or slow-reveal subplot can keep your show sticky. Think *The Good Place*'s season-long twist, *Arrested Development*'s hidden jokes, or *BoJack Horseman*'s emotional arcs buried under gags.

Ways to layer depth:

- A character's past keeps surfacing in absurd ways.
- A running lie begins to spiral out of control.
- A background character slowly rises into focus.

Use ChatGPT to help:

"What's a subtle subplot I can plant in Season 1 of a comedy that could pay off in Season 3?"

4. Design Plot Structures That Can Vary

To stay fresh, you need episodic *and* serialized storylines. You want to be able to:

- Tell stand-alone stories for casual viewers.
- Build season arcs for loyal fans.
- Include bottle episodes, experimental formats, or genre homages.

Ask ChatGPT to test variety:

"List 10 different episode formats for a comedy series set in a family-run hotel. Include at least one flashback, one dream sequence, and one real-time episode."

If your show is too rigid, it gets old fast. Build variety into the bones.

5. Let Relationships Evolve Organically

The key to multiple seasons isn't new plots—it's shifting dynamics. Friends become rivals. Rivals become allies. A romantic arc might stall, break, or finally deliver. The important thing is that nothing stays frozen.

Keep emotional tension alive with:

- Will-they-won't-they plots that get disrupted.
- Power shifts between coworkers, friends, or families.
- Loyalty vs. ambition, idealism vs. compromise, change vs. comfort.

Ask:

"How can I stretch a love-hate dynamic across three seasons without making it repetitive?"

ChatGPT can map arcs that zig where the audience expects a zag.

6. Plan for Fresh Characters and Fresh Stakes

New characters are like new spices—if the core cast is solid, adding one or two can revitalize the mix. But they have to serve a purpose:

- A new rival, ally, or wildcard.
- A generational contrast.
- A threat to the status quo.

At the same time, raise the stakes each season—but don't break the tone. A promotion, a move, a scandal, a secret revealed—these changes should challenge characters, not reset them.

Prompt:

"Design a character who joins in Season 2 and disrupts a tight-knit trio dynamic without replacing anyone."

7. Know When to Let Characters Fail or Win

Sometimes the funniest, most powerful thing you can do for your show is let a character *actually get what they want*—and realize it's not what they thought. Or let them lose and find themselves in a new kind of trouble. Real comedy sustains when wins and losses feel like they matter.

Great long-term comedy is built on that push and pull:

- Michael Scott gets the office to like him—right before he leaves it.
- Leslie Knope wins an election—and immediately faces a worse job.
- Fleabag finds connection—then has to let it go.

Ask ChatGPT:

"What's a Season 2 climax that gives a character what they want, but in a way that's funny, bittersweet, and reveals they weren't ready for it?"

8. Plant Seeds for Seasons Ahead

If you know you want your show to last, start planting early. Don't overload the pilot—but seed possibilities:

- A throwaway line about a parent or ex.
- A character's secret hobby that could become a major plot point.
- A missed opportunity that keeps coming back.

Callbacks, slow burns, hidden setups—they all make later seasons feel earned.

Use:

"List five small background details I can plant in Season 1 that could become major storylines later."

Comedy that lasts isn't afraid to shift. It lets its world expand, its characters grow (or dig in), and its rhythm change just enough to stay alive. You're not just writing to make people laugh now—you're writing to make them laugh *again*, later, louder, and with more meaning.

So dream past the pilot. Write scenes that build memory. Make every episode funny, but let every season matter.

Because a great comedy show doesn't just survive past one season.

It *deserves* to.

Keeping Characters Funny Without Making Them Static

One of the biggest traps in long-running comedy is this: keeping a character funny by keeping them exactly the same. At first, it works. Audiences love consistency—especially when the traits are extreme. The guy who always panics. The woman who always over-prepares. The boss who can't stop misusing words. But after a season or two? Predictability kills surprise. Surprise is the oxygen of comedy. And without it, even the best character becomes a parody of themselves.

So how do you keep your characters funny *and* fresh—without flattening them into sitcom punch machines? You let them grow... but not too fast. You evolve them without sanding off the parts that make them hilarious. You deepen the contradiction at their core.

Let's break that down.

1. Don't Change Who They Are—Change What They're Facing

Your character's personality can stay the same—but the *context* around them should keep shifting. A control freak is funny when they're trying to run a meeting—but funnier when they're in a wilderness survival class. A people pleaser is funny when they're catering a party—but funnier when they're asked to fire someone.

By changing the *situation*, not the personality, you let the character stay consistent while the comedy stays unpredictable.

Try this with ChatGPT:

"Give me five increasingly absurd situations for a character who's obsessed with being liked by everyone, even their enemies."

2. Let Characters Learn... and Then Forget

Real people don't learn perfectly. They change in fits and starts. They relapse. They backslide. They make the same mistakes in new ways. That's where the comedy comes in.

Example:

- In Season 1, the character avoids conflict by lying.
- In Season 2, they *try* honesty—but it goes badly, so they double down on passive-aggressive gift-giving instead.
- In Season 3, they join a "truth-telling" workshop and accidentally destroy three relationships in one week.

You're not forcing them to "grow up"—you're letting them *try*. That's funny.

Use ChatGPT to structure:

"Outline a three-season arc where a know-it-all character slowly becomes more self-aware—but keeps using their awareness to prove they were right all along."

3. Introduce New Sides without Abandoning the Core

If a character is always angry, show what happens when they try yoga. If a jokester is never serious, let them fail at giving a toast. These moments reveal new dimensions—but they're still rooted in the original flaw.

Ask yourself:

- What's something this character would *never* do... until now?
- What's a situation where their usual tactic doesn't work?
- What's a side of them even they don't realize exists?

Then let the comedy come from the struggle to *reconcile* those parts—not from becoming someone new.

Ask ChatGPT:

"Write a scene where a gruff, emotionally closed-off character accidentally gives great advice and can't deal with the gratitude."

4. Keep Character Dynamics in Motion

A great way to keep characters funny is by changing how they bounce off *each other*. A duo where one is the straight man and the other the clown might flip for an episode. Or maybe a side character becomes a temporary leader, and the usual alpha has to follow.

Shake up:

- Power dynamics
- Emotional dependencies
- Odd-couple pairings
- Trust and betrayal (in funny ways)

Try ChatGPT:

"Give me five episodes where a comic duo is forced into new roles—like switching jobs, personalities, or goals—for fresh comedy."

5. Use Running Gags to Reinforce, Not Replace

Running gags are great—but don't let them become a crutch. If a character is known for one catchphrase or behavior, it *has* to evolve or surprise.

For example:

- First: The character says "Nailed it!" after every failure.
- Later: They start saying it before doing anything.
- Season Finale: They say "Nailed it!" *accurately* for once—and it's weirdly moving.

Let the gag reflect their journey. Or let someone else co-opt it. Or turn it against them.

Use ChatGPT:

"Suggest a way to evolve a catchphrase across three seasons so it becomes emotionally meaningful and still funny."

6. Track Internal Contradictions

This is the secret to long-term character comedy: contradiction. A person who's terrified of attention but craves validation. Someone who thinks they're the hero but is clearly the chaos agent. As long as the character contains a live, unresolved contradiction, they'll always be funny.

Keep a list of:

- What they say vs. what they do
- What they want vs. what they actually need
- What they fear most—and how they avoid it (badly)

These contradictions are wells you can draw from forever. Especially when a new situation puts pressure on the exact part they thought they'd hidden.

Try:

"Build a character who says they're emotionally evolved but can't handle being unfollowed on social media."

7. Let Them Surprise Themselves

The funniest, most human thing a character can do is *shock even themselves*. Let them say, "I can't believe I just said that," or "Who am I right now?" These moments give both the audience and the character permission to explore. It's not just character growth—it's comic elasticity.

Use ChatGPT to explore this:

"Write a moment where a character finally says what they've been holding in for years, and it comes out completely wrong, but totally cathartic."

Funny doesn't mean frozen. You don't have to choose between writing jokes and writing depth. When a character stays true to their core flaw, tries (and fails) to grow, and faces new challenges with old habits, they stay endlessly funny. And more importantly—they stay alive. Your job isn't to protect your characters from change. It's to *trap them inside it*, hand them a shovel, and watch them dig the hole deeper—with a punchline.

Next, we'll talk about how to land a **series finale** that honors this evolution, delivers the biggest laughs, and leaves your audience with the perfect blend of closure and "just one more joke."

Writing a Series Finale That Delivers Laughs and Closure

Ending a comedy series is one of the trickiest balancing acts in writing. You want to go out with a bang, but not a scream. You want your audience laughing—maybe even crying—but most of all, *satisfied*. The finale has to feel like the show's natural endpoint, not just another episode with "The End" slapped on. It needs to wrap up arcs, deliver full-circle jokes, honor character journeys, and—yes—still be funny.

Great comedy finales don't abandon the tone that made the series work. Instead, they *elevate* it. They take the same ingredients and cook the best meal of the series. So how do you do that?

Let's explore how to create a finale that delivers on both emotional payoff and the laughs your audience has come to expect.

1. Decide: Are You Ending the Story, or the Show?

Some comedies end the *plot*. Others end the *vibe*. Your finale needs to know what it's aiming for.

- *Plot-driven finales* resolve a central question: Will they move? Will they break up? Will the job end?
- *Character-driven finales* are about emotional closure: Who have these people become? What have they learned, if anything?

Think of *The Good Place* (high-concept closure), *Schitt's Creek* (romantic and familial payoff), or *New Girl* (a silly, warm look forward).

Ask ChatGPT:

"Outline a character-based finale for a show about three roommates who still don't have their lives together, but are finally okay with it."

2. Bring the Story (or Stories) Full Circle

The best finales nod to the beginning—not in a forced way, but in a reflective, satisfying one. Let early jokes, situations, or settings return in new forms. The callback becomes the reward.

Ideas:

- The very first disagreement comes back in a different light.
- An old lie is finally exposed—only for nobody to care anymore.
- A place they hated now feels like home.

Try this:

"Help me turn a joke from Season 1 into a heartfelt moment in the series finale—without making it too sentimental."

3. Give Every Character a Moment (But Not a Monologue)

A satisfying finale gives each character one last spotlight. It doesn't mean giving them a speech—it means giving them a *choice*. Something that reflects their arc or contradiction.

Examples:

- The commitment-phobe finally admits they care—but messes it up anyway.
- The control freak lets someone else make the plan (then tries to fix it quietly).
- The loner joins the group picture without being asked.

ChatGPT prompt:

"List closing beats for five comedic characters that show growth but keep their personality intact."

This isn't about fixing them. It's about showing who they are *now*, compared to who they were.

4. Keep the Comedy Coming—Even in the Goodbyes

The ending can be emotional, but it must still be funny. The key? Let the characters *stay themselves* while going through change.

- They ruin their own goodbye party.
- Someone turns a heartfelt toast into a therapy session.
- They accidentally leave someone behind—and don't notice for hours.

Use ChatGPT:

"Write a farewell scene where a character tries to leave dramatically, but keeps forgetting things and has to come back."

Comedy keeps the finale from turning into a funeral. And a well-timed gag after an emotional beat? That's where the magic is.

5. Deliver One Final Surprise

A great finale gives you *one thing* you didn't expect—but when it happens, you realize it was inevitable.

- A silent character finally says something meaningful.
- A background gag pays off in a huge way.
- A pair you never thought would connect finally do—in a totally bizarre but moving way.

Ask:

"Pitch a final twist for a workplace comedy that doesn't change the tone but adds a new layer to everything that came before."

You want the audience to feel: "Oh. *Of course.*"

6. Let Them Go… But Leave the Door Open

You don't have to kill the story. Sometimes just *pausing* the world works better. Suggest the next chapter without writing it.

- Characters scatter—but the text thread keeps going.

- One character stays behind, smiling like they know they'll be okay.
- A final freeze frame. A final inside joke. A final callback.

Use ChatGPT:

"Write a last scene that suggests these characters will be okay even if we never see them again."

7. Echo the First Episode—But Evolved

A great finale often mirrors the pilot. This could be:

- A similar situation with different reactions.
- A reversed dynamic.
- A line repeated—but with new meaning.

Example:

Pilot: "We're not friends. We're roommates."

Finale: "We were never just roommates."

It hits because we *earned* the shift.

Ask:

"What's a line from a pilot that could return in the finale with emotional weight and humor?"

Final Thought

Writing a comedy finale isn't about proving how clever you are. It's about proving how *much these characters mattered*—without losing the tone that made us fall for them in the first place. It's not about ending every storyline. It's about closing the curtain on *this* chapter of the story, with enough truth, absurdity, and laughter to remind the audience why they loved this world in the first place.

Make them laugh. Make them feel. Then leave them with one last beat they'll carry in their head like a favorite line they'll never forget.

Because that's what a great finale does. It doesn't say goodbye. It says, "You'll think of us when you need to laugh again."

And that? That's the perfect final punchline.

Revisiting Past Episodes for Continuity and Running Gags

If you're building a comedy series that lasts more than a season—or even just writing a tight, cohesive single season—then continuity isn't just a detail. It's part of the joke. Callbacks, running gags, emotional through-lines, character arcs, and in-universe logic are what make a show feel like a living, breathing world. And revisiting past episodes—on purpose—lets you reinforce the funny, reward loyal viewers, and deepen the humor without stretching for new material every time.

This chapter is about how to use your *own history*—your own previous episodes—as creative raw material. Not just for consistency, but for payoff. For evolution. For turning a throwaway bit from Episode 2 into a fan-favorite in Episode 8.

Let's dive in.

1. Continuity Is a Tool, Not a Trap

You don't have to be perfect. This isn't sci-fi. A missed date or mismatched outfit won't break your show. But emotional continuity and joke logic? Those matter.

- If a character hated dogs in Episode 3, don't make them run a dog-walking business in Episode 6 without comment.
- If a character failed their driving test in Season 1, and suddenly they're confidently parallel parking in Season 2—*at least* make it a joke.

You want the world to feel alive, not reset.

Try using ChatGPT to audit for consistency:

"Summarize all facts we've established about this character's childhood/family/quirks over ten episodes."

2. Running Gags: Plant Early, Build Slowly, Pay Off Big

A running gag works best when:

- It's established clearly and simply.
- It comes back unexpectedly.
- It escalates or evolves over time.

Example:

- Episode 1: A character claims they have a PhD in "Conflict Resolution."
- Episode 4: They try to mediate a fight and make it worse.
- Episode 9: Someone sarcastically gives them a fake diploma during an apology.

Use ChatGPT to design a running gag:

"Create a recurring character trait that starts small but can build into a full scene by the end of the season."

Let the gag *breathe* between episodes so it surprises the audience when it returns.

3. Revisit Earlier Scenes from a New Perspective

This is a great way to build story depth and squeeze out more laughs. Let later episodes reframe earlier ones:

- What if a flashback shows that an emotional speech was plagiarized?
- What if the "heroic" act we saw in Episode 2 was totally misunderstood?
- What if a minor background character from Episode 1 turns out to have a huge grudge?

Prompt:

"Give me five episode ideas that reinterpret events from earlier in the season from a different character's perspective."

This technique works best when it's subtle—and hilarious. It keeps fans rewatching.

4. Tie Character Reactions to Past Events

A key way to maintain continuity and deepen comedy is to let your characters *remember* what happened to them—and act accordingly.

Examples:

- A character who was betrayed in Episode 5 brings it up every time there's a group vote.
- A phobia introduced early on resurfaces in weird, inappropriate ways.
- A character who got left out of a plan once now assumes they're being excluded all the time.

Ask ChatGPT:

"Write a scene where a character overreacts to a simple request because of something that happened in Episode 3."

This builds emotional continuity without losing laughs. It rewards the viewer's memory.

5. Bring Back Props, Locations, and Background Bits

World-building isn't just in the lines. Objects, places, and even set decorations can return for comic effect.

Examples:

- A suspicious smoothie machine becomes a running source of minor disasters.
- A wall of passive-aggressive "Employee of the Month" photos starts including pets.
- A background extra slowly gets more involved with each episode, until they're part of the team.

Use ChatGPT to generate:

"List background gags that could build quietly across a season, then pay off big in the finale."

These visual gags create layered storytelling—and make rewatches extra fun.

6. Use Character Vocabulary as a Continuity Shortcut

Every character has a way of speaking—certain phrases, metaphors, or catchwords. If they stick to them over time, it builds comic identity and helps you plant mini-callbacks without needing full scenes.

Examples:

- One character always calls bad ideas "bold strategies."
- Another refers to every setback as "a test from the universe."
- A third keeps inventing fake idioms like "Well, butter my tennis racket."

Let ChatGPT help build a language profile:

"Give me five signature phrases or expressions for a character who's overly confident but always wrong."

7. Turn Loose Threads into Future Gold

Every comedy writer leaves behind unused setups, weird details, or jokes that didn't go anywhere. You can mine them later.

Look through past scripts for:

- One-liners that hint at a bigger story ("That's almost as bad as the raccoon situation last year...")
- Background characters with strange energy.
- Visual gags you never explained.

Then ask:

"What's a full episode I could build out of this small joke from Episode 2?"

Let the audience feel like you've had the whole plan from day one—even if you're just catching up now.

Final Thought

Revisiting past episodes isn't about making your show airtight. It's about making it *cohesive*. It's about finding the narrative thread in your own mess, the echo in your own laughter. When you build continuity on purpose, every joke lands harder. Every callback feels earned. Every moment becomes part of something bigger—even if it started as a throwaway line.

So don't just write forward. Look back. The funniest thing in your finale might be hiding in your pilot.

How to Use ChatGPT to Break a Story in Real Time

One of the most magical (and intimidating) parts of writing a comedy series is breaking the story—figuring out what actually happens in the episode. What's the setup? What's the turning point? What's the hilarious disaster? Where does it end, and how does it echo something deeper? In a traditional writers' room, story-breaking happens on whiteboards and couches, with people shouting ideas until a structure clicks. But when you're writing solo, or on a deadline, or just trying to get *something* on the page, breaking story in real time with ChatGPT can be the fastest, smartest creative partner in the room.

Here's how to do it.

1. Start With a Vague Idea—Then Talk It Out

Begin with the most basic fragment: a setting, a character moment, a funny conflict. You don't need a full logline or outline. You just need a vibe.

Example:

"I want to write an episode where one of the roommates lies about knowing how to salsa dance to impress a date."

That's it. That's your seed. ChatGPT can help you expand:

"Help me break a 22-minute comedy episode around this idea. What's the setup, escalation, midpoint disaster, and resolution?"

You'll get a rough roadmap in seconds—beats you can shape and challenge in real time.

2. Workshop the Beats One by One

Once you have a general shape, zoom in. Break the episode into five to seven major beats and go beat-by-beat, using ChatGPT to explore options, generate alternate paths, and find funnier angles.

Try:

"In Beat 2, the character agrees to enter a salsa contest. What are three ways this moment could be escalated for comedy?"

Or:

"What's an unexpected way for the salsa lie to get exposed that could happen in a public setting?"

Use ChatGPT to *riff* with you. You'll find that story-breaking becomes a conversation rather than a chore.

3. Create Character-Based Versions of the Same Plot

ChatGPT can help you run variations of the same story through different character lenses.

Ask:

"What would this salsa plot look like if the lying character was the confident narcissist of the group? What if it were the anxious people-pleaser?"

Now you're not just breaking one story—you're testing who it *belongs* to, and who can make it funniest.

4. Test Reversals and Heightening Options in Real Time

A great story beat surprises. ChatGPT can help you "yes, and" your way to better twists and reversals.

Prompt:

"What's a twist ending for this story that still feels earned—but totally flips the character's goal?"

Or:

"How can we escalate this lie beyond a dance contest—without losing plausibility?"

Even if you reject half the ideas, the back-and-forth gets you where you need to go faster than pacing your kitchen floor.

5. Lock In Subplots and Thematic Echoes

Once you've got the main arc, let ChatGPT help you shape a B-story or C-story that complements the theme.

Try:

"What's a subplot for another roommate that plays off the theme of pretending to be someone you're not?"

Or:

"Suggest three visual gags or small moments that can echo the salsa lie without being part of the main plot."

These small echoes build cohesion and comedy throughout the episode.

6. Create an Episode Beat Sheet in Seconds

Once you've locked in the big beats, ask:

"Turn this episode breakdown into a clear beat sheet I can follow while writing the script."

You'll get:

- Cold open
- Act One structure
- Midpoint twist
- Escalation
- Final gag or emotional beat

Now your blueprint is ready—and you didn't spend five hours staring at a blinking cursor.

7. Use ChatGPT to Rewrite and Re-Break

Story breaking isn't linear. You'll hit walls. You'll get new ideas mid-dialogue. That's okay.

Prompt:

"Actually, I want the date character to be a dance instructor. How would that change the structure of the story?"

Or:

"I need a new ending. Something low-key, funny, and honest that doesn't require a big public moment."

In a writers' room, this is called "breaking it again." With ChatGPT, you can do it in minutes, not days.

Breaking a story is messy, unpredictable, and full of wrong turns—and that's what makes it fun. With ChatGPT in the room, you don't have to wait for inspiration or a collaborator. You can riff, reshape, escalate, and twist in real time. You can test every "what if" without second-guessing or losing momentum.

You're not using ChatGPT to *replace* the writers' room. You're using it to *simulate* the energy of one—on demand, on your schedule, and always ready to throw out another idea.

Speedwriting a Comedy Episode with AI in One Sitting

So, you've broken the story. You've mapped the beats. You know your characters, their quirks, their issues, and their signature punchlines. Now comes the wild part: writing the actual episode. The full 22-page comedy script. And instead of slogging through it over two or three weeks, you're going to do it *today*. In one sitting. With help.

This is speedwriting with ChatGPT. It's fast. It's focused. And it works because it's not about perfection—it's about momentum. You're not writing the *final* version. You're creating a hilarious, structured, story-driven *draft*—and letting AI help keep your brain out of your way.

Here's your game plan.

1. Start with Your Beat Sheet (or Get One Quickly)

Before you write a single line of dialogue, you need a roadmap. If you already broke your story, perfect. If not, prompt ChatGPT to help create one:

"Give me a beat sheet for a 22-minute sitcom episode about a character who lies about having a twin brother to impress a love interest."

You'll get something like:

- Cold open: awkward intro, mistaken identity
- Act One: the lie spirals
- Act Two: someone meets the "twin"
- Act Three: reveal, fallout, forgiveness (sort of)
- Tag: joke payoff or ironic button

Save this. It's your skeleton.

2. Set a Timer and Write Scene by Scene

Now you're going to work in focused sprints. Use ChatGPT to help write one scene at a time—then *move on*.

Prompt:

"Write the cold open of this sitcom episode: Character A lies about having a twin to impress a love interest. Keep it short, visual, and funny."

You'll get a first draft of the scene. You can tweak it as needed, or just accept and keep going. The point isn't to make it perfect—the point is to get the scene *down*.

Then move on:

"Now write the next scene where the roommate finds out about the lie and demands to play the fake twin."

Continue like this, scene by scene. Each new prompt builds on the last. If a scene stalls, ask for variations:

"Give me a version of this scene where the love interest almost discovers the truth but gets distracted."

3. Use Character Voice Shortcuts

To keep each scene funny and consistent, remind ChatGPT of your characters' voices:

"Character A is anxious and talks too much. Character B is dry and deadpan. Rewrite this scene with their distinct voices."

You can also keep a running "character profile" in a side window or document to paste back into prompts if ChatGPT starts drifting.

4. Keep the Momentum over Polish

You're aiming for a complete, readable episode draft—not the final version. Resist the urge to go back and perfect jokes or fix every beat. Stay in motion.

Think: first table read, not final shoot.

If you get stuck, prompt:

"Give me three ways to transition out of this awkward reveal and into the next beat where they prepare the twin costume."

5. Add Jokes, Tags, and Punch-Ups On the Fly

Once you have a scene down, ask ChatGPT to help punch it up:

"Punch up this scene with funnier dialogue and at least two callbacks to earlier jokes."

"Give this scene a stronger button—a final line that lands the laugh before the cut."

This is your room rewrite—quick, flexible, and focused on *heightening*.

6. Generate the Full Script in a Clean Format

Once you've written every scene (likely 8–10 total for a 22-minute show), ask ChatGPT to stitch it together:

"Combine these scenes into a single formatted comedy script with scene headings and character names in proper script format."

Or use:

"Format this as a 22-minute sitcom script using industry-standard formatting. Include a cold open, three acts, and a tag scene."

Paste it into your screenwriting software later for polish, but this version gives you a clear view of the whole draft *now*.

7. Add Episode Title, Logline, and One-Sentence Pitch

Once you've got the episode written, you can generate the supporting materials for pitching or submitting.

Ask:

"Based on this script, what's a clever episode title?"

"Write a one-sentence logline for this episode."

"Summarize this episode in three lines for a pitch deck."

Now you're not just writing fast—you're *producing* like a pro.

Speedwriting isn't about cutting corners. It's about giving yourself permission to write *before you talk yourself out of it.* When you team up with ChatGPT, you get the energy of a full writers' room compressed into a single, focused writing sprint. You're building something you can revise, elevate, and refine—but you're *building it today.*

So block off a few hours. Pour some coffee. Let your imagination take the wheel. And remember: the secret to writing a funny episode in one sitting isn't pressure.

It's *momentum.*

Polishing a First Draft until It's Prime Time Ready

You did it—you wrote a comedy episode. It's funny. It's structured. It has character beats, jokes that actually land, and maybe even a surprise emotional moment that sneaked in without your permission. But now comes the part that separates the "wrote an episode" crowd from the "this could actually get made" crowd: the polish.

Polishing a first draft is where a script goes from good to *tight*. It's where the rhythm clicks, the jokes sing, the dialogue sounds human, and every page earns its space. It's not about rewriting from scratch—it's about sharpening, clarifying, and making sure *everything works together*.

With ChatGPT as your sidekick, polishing your comedy script doesn't have to be overwhelming. In fact, it can be fast, focused, and even fun—like a final table read with a hyper-caffeinated writers' room.

Here's how to do it.

1. Read it like an Audience, Not a Writer

Before touching a line, read the whole script through—out loud, if possible. Note:

- Where you laugh.
- Where you *don't* laugh but wanted to.
- Where scenes feel long or lose energy.
- Where transitions feel abrupt or flat.
- Where characters suddenly sound off.

Then use ChatGPT like a mirror:

"Summarize this scene in one sentence. Does it have clear conflict and resolution?"

"Does this character sound consistent with how I described them earlier?"

"Does this line read funnier if it's trimmed or reversed?"

You're not rewriting yet. You're *listening*.

2. Cut Flab, Add Punch

In comedy, shorter is almost always better. Every extra word, every unnecessary line, every slow setup can kill the rhythm.

Use ChatGPT to tighten:

"Rewrite this paragraph of dialogue to keep the character's voice but make it 30% shorter."

"Punch up this monologue to be snappier and land with a stronger button."

Remember, your goal isn't just clarity—it's *speed*. Keep the pacing quick, even when the stakes are high.

3. Heighten the Jokes That Already Work

You've got good jokes. Now make them great.

Try:

"This line gets a chuckle. Give me five punch-up versions—one wordier, one darker, one absurd, one callback, one silent beat alternative."

"What's a physical gag that could replace this line and get a laugh without dialogue?"

Even a good punchline might hit harder if the *setup* is rewritten. Ask:

"How can I rewrite this setup so the punchline lands harder without changing the joke?"

4. Use Rhythm Edits for Flow and Voice

Each character should sound like *themself*. Even if you're writing fast, now's the time to polish each voice.

Prompt:

"Character A talks in motivational clichés but doesn't know what they mean. Character B is sarcastic and deadpan. Rewrite this scene to reflect their distinct voices."

Also try:

"Make this dialogue more rhythmic, with better comic timing and short pauses built in for performance."

A good rhythm edit makes the scene read *like it will play*.

5. Polish Scene Transitions and Visual Beats

The space between scenes matters. Avoid hard cuts that confuse the viewer or jokes that land but don't *lead* anywhere.

Ask:

"Does this scene transition logically and clearly into the next, or should there be a bridging line or beat?"

"Suggest a visual gag or prop-based action that could end this scene on a laugh instead of a fade out."

6. Punch Up the Cold Open and Final Tag

The cold open sets the tone. The tag is the final impression. These need to land strong.

Use ChatGPT:

"This cold open is okay. How could I make it riskier, sharper, or more character-driven?"

"Give me five alternate tag jokes that callback to earlier episodes or character flaws."

Don't be afraid to *rewrite just these sections* from scratch—they're often the easiest parts to boost.

7. Fix Formatting and Clarity

Don't let a great script get buried in clutter or confusion. Use AI to clean:

"Format this as a sitcom script with standard scene headings, action lines, and character names."

"Scan this script for repeated lines, overused phrases, or unclear blocking."

Keep it easy to read. Fast turns pages. Confusion kills interest.

8. Test It Scene by Scene with AI Table Reads

Simulate a table read:

"Read this scene aloud as Character A (chaotic optimist), Character B (dry realist), and Character C (nervous over-sharer). Emphasize tone, pacing, and joke rhythm."

You'll quickly spot:

- Who gets too many lines.
- Who needs a punchline.
- Which beats drag.

Use this to rebalance scenes.

9. Track the Callbacks and Emotional Echoes

Make sure any running gags or emotional threads *pay off.* If you set it up, land it.

Ask:

"Which setups in this episode are missing callbacks or emotional echoes?"

"Suggest a final moment that ties back to the character's journey in a funny but satisfying way."

This is where your script becomes a *story*, not just a collection of scenes.

10. Trust the Weird—But Justify It

If something's weird but funny? Great. If it's weird and confusing? Fix it.

Prompt:

"This moment is surreal and strange—how can I make it feel grounded in the character's logic?"

"Give me a justification for this bizarre moment that could be played straight."

Weirdness works *if it's earned.*

A polished script doesn't sparkle because it's clever. It sparkles because it's *clear*. Because it *knows what it is.* And because it was made with love—for the characters, the world, and the people who'll laugh at it. Polishing with ChatGPT means you're never alone in the rewrite. You've got a scene partner, a comedy doctor, a story analyst, and a joke machine right beside you. Use that power—but always keep your voice at the center. You're not fixing the script. You're *finishing the show.*

Creating a Demo Script to Pitch Your Comedy Series

So you've written a comedy script. Maybe you even have a few episodes drafted. You've laughed, rewritten, polished—and now you're ready to do something with it. You want to get it read. Get it noticed. Get it *sold.* This is where your demo script comes in. It's your calling card, your proof of concept, your "this is what my show is" moment. And it has one job: make someone laugh *and* want more.

A great demo script doesn't just show that you can write. It shows that you can build a *series.* It shows voice, character, structure, and commercial viability—all wrapped in a 22- to 30-page document that feels both complete and like the beginning of something bigger.

Let's walk through how to create a demo script that's not just good—but pitch-ready.

1. Choose the Right Episode to Demo

Your demo script doesn't always have to be the pilot. In fact, sometimes the pilot is too setup-heavy. Many successful pitches use Episode 2 or 3 as the writing sample, letting the pilot act as a series bible and background doc.

So ask yourself:

- Does the pilot feel like a satisfying episode on its own?
- Does another episode better reflect the voice, rhythm, and tone of your series?
- Is there an episode that showcases all of your main characters and your core comedic energy?

Ask ChatGPT:

"Help me choose between these three episode ideas for a demo script—consider which one introduces the world, delivers laughs, and shows off character dynamics best."

If you only have one episode written, no problem. Just make sure it's your strongest possible showcase.

2. Make It Standalone—But With a Series Feel

Your demo script should work on its own. It should have a clear conflict, escalation, and resolution. But it should also *hint* at a larger world.

Include:

- Clear character voices and dynamics.
- At least one running gag or recurring beat that could echo through a season.
- A final moment that feels like either an emotional or comedic payoff—and ideally, both.

You can let ChatGPT scan for standalone strength:

"Does this script resolve its central conflict and still leave room for more stories? Suggest changes to make it feel more complete as a sample."

3. Show the Show's Rhythm and Voice

Anyone reading your script is also imagining the show it belongs to. Use the episode to convey:

- The tone (broad? grounded? absurd? heartfelt?)
- The pacing (snappy? slow-burn? chaotic energy?)
- The world (stylized? realistic? heightened-but-relatable?)

Try:

"Rewrite this scene with the pacing and voice of a modern single-cam comedy like *Abbott Elementary*."

Or

"Punch up this beat so it reflects the offbeat, surreal humor of *Search Party*."

You want the reader to *feel* the show—even if they never see the pitch deck.

4. Start Strong—End Stronger

The first page sells the read. The last page sells the show.

The cold open should do three things:

- Introduce a character or dynamic.
- Make us laugh.
- Establish tone.

The final page should:

- Deliver a comedic or emotional payoff.
- Show growth (or an earned lack of it).
- Leave us wanting the *next* episode.

Ask ChatGPT:

"Give me five stronger cold opens for this character-based comedy pilot."

"Suggest a better final beat that lands the theme and keeps it funny."

5. Format like a Pro

Industry-standard formatting isn't optional. Your demo script should read like a script someone could hand to a cast and crew tomorrow.

Use:

- Correct scene headings (INT./EXT., DAY/NIGHT)
- Clean character name blocks
- Action lines that are short, visual, and clear

- Dialogue (centered under Character's name) that's well-spaced and punchy

Ask:

"Check this script for formatting errors. Are the scene headings and dialogue lines consistent with TV comedy standards?"

Better yet, paste the entire script into screenwriting software like Final Draft, Celtx, or WriterDuet for that final polish.

6. Add a Short Logline and Series Blurb

When you send your script, include a one-page summary that contains:

- The title
- A one-sentence logline (clear, funny, high-concept or high-character)
- A paragraph that describes the world, tone, and central dynamic of the show

Example:

Title: *Wrong Number*

Logline: After answering a call meant for someone else, an anxious data analyst pretends to be a life coach—and accidentally builds a cult following.

Series Summary: Set in a world of self-help nonsense, office dysfunction, and growing social media madness, *Wrong Number* is a half-hour comedy about imposter syndrome, accidental fame, and the lies we tell when we really need a win.

ChatGPT can help you draft it:

"Write a one-page pitch summary and logline for my comedy pilot based on this episode."

7. Know What Makes It *Yours*

Your demo script is your voice. Your take. Your brand of funny. Make sure it sounds like *you*—not like a generic "TV comedy writer."

Ask:

"What's a signature trait of my writing style in this script? How can I bring that out more?"

"Where could I add more of my comedic perspective without being too 'writerly' or show-offy?"

The more your demo script feels *specific*, the more it feels *professional.*

A demo script isn't just a writing sample. It's a proof of concept. It's your "I can write a show" credential. It should feel like an invitation to an entire world—and when someone finishes it, they should be wondering what happens next, who else is in the cast, and how soon they can get it on screen. So take the time to polish it. Tighten it. Own it. Let it be the script that doesn't just say "I'm funny." Let it say, "I'm ready."

What Producers and Streamers Want in a Comedy Series Now

You've got the script. You've got the pitch. You've even got a catchy title that's screaming to be turned into a series. But now comes the big question: will someone *buy* it? Will a producer, executive, or streamer read your comedy and say, "This is exactly what we're looking for"? The answer depends on more than whether it's funny. These days, buyers want comedy that's not just entertaining—but *strategic*. Something that fits the current market, aligns with the brand, and offers something fresh without being a complete risk.

Let's break down what producers and streaming platforms are *actually* looking for in comedy series right now—and how you can tailor your pitch to deliver it.

1. A Unique POV—But Broad Appeal

Executives want to feel like they're hearing a voice they've never heard before. But they also want that voice to connect with a wide audience.

This means:

- Stories from underrepresented perspectives *with universal emotion.*
- Specific cultures, subcultures, or worlds that haven't been overdone.
- Humor that's authentic, but still accessible to people outside the world it depicts.

Example: *Ramy*, *Mo*, *Derry Girls*, and *Reservation Dogs* all start from distinct identities—but explore love, guilt, family, and purpose in ways anyone can feel.

Ask ChatGPT:

"Help me describe my comedy show's perspective in a way that emphasizes what makes it unique and broadly relatable."

2. Character-Driven, Not Concept-Dependent

While high-concept comedies (*Upload*, *The Good Place*) still get attention, the real gold lies in *character engines.* Buyers want characters who:

- Can generate new stories every episode.
- Have flaws that drive conflict and comedy.
- Feel fresh without needing a new gimmick each season.

If your show only works because of a single idea ("What if your dog could talk?"), it might not last. But if your show works because the characters *never stop making bad decisions for emotionally understandable reasons*—now you've got something.

Ask:

"What makes my characters story engines? Help me write a paragraph explaining how their personalities drive every episode."

3. Streamable Structure—But Not Formulaic

Streamers want comedy that binge-watches well. That means:

- Strong cold opens to hook viewers immediately.
- Narrative threads or arcs that reward sequential viewing.
- Episodes that are short, punchy, and leave a little something hanging.

Even if your show is mostly episodic, they'll want some continuity or progression (a slow-burn romance, a brewing rivalry, a secret, etc.) to keep people clicking "Next Episode."

ChatGPT can help:

"Help me rewrite this season arc summary to make it feel binge-worthy without becoming a drama."

4. Format Flexibility

Today's comedy isn't always 22 minutes or a traditional three-act sitcom. Streamers are open to:

- 10–30 minute episodes depending on tone.
- Single-cam over multi-cam (most of the time).
- Hybrid formats (mockumentary, surreal realism, animated-adjacent).
- Shows that can be short-run or mini-series format.

If your show can adapt to either limited or long-run storytelling, say so. Flexibility is attractive to networks juggling shifting budgets and audience attention spans.

Prompt:

"Frame my 8-episode comedy season as a mini-series that leaves room for additional seasons or spin-offs."

5. A Hook beyond the Page

Producers love shows that can *sell themselves*—not just with a good script, but with a strong concept, title, and logline.

Your pitch should clearly convey:

- What the show *is*—in 1–2 sentences.
- Why it *matters*—now.
- Why it's *you*—why you're the person to tell it.

If the reader can't repeat your show's premise without reading the pitch doc again, it's too murky.

Ask ChatGPT:

"Help me write a logline that a producer can repeat in a meeting after hearing it once."

6. Built-In Audience or Social Relevance (Optional, but Powerful)

Streamers *love* if there's a way to build buzz:

- Does the show reflect a community or cultural trend that's growing?
- Does the creator have a platform or following?
- Is the topic something people are already debating, sharing, or posting memes about?

This isn't essential—but if your show naturally connects to something that's hot right now (without being forced), use it to your advantage.

Prompt:

"Frame my show about friendship and freelancing as something relevant to Gen Z and millennial work culture."

7. Proof It Can Be Made (and for What Budget)

More than ever, producers want to know your show is *feasible*—especially with shrinking production budgets. If your story mostly takes place in a few locations and focuses on dialogue and performance over set pieces, lean into that.

Don't hide limitations—sell them as advantages:

- "It's mostly one location with five speaking roles—perfect for a tight budget."
- "No special effects or expensive sequences—just pure character comedy."

Use ChatGPT to phrase it:

"Write a paragraph pitching the low-budget appeal of this high-concept comedy idea."

What producers and streamers want isn't a mystery. They want what audiences want—*comedy that feels fresh, relatable, and worth spending time with.* But they also want comedy that's ready to move: shows that are castable, producible, bingeable, and repeatable.

Your job isn't just to make them laugh—it's to make them *believe.* That this story, with these characters, in this tone, could be the next thing people are quoting, sharing, and re-watching.

Building a Portfolio of Comedy with the Help of AI

If you're serious about working in comedy—whether as a writer, showrunner, creator, or punch-up artist—you need more than just one great script. You need a *portfolio*: a collection of writing samples that shows your range, your voice, and your ability to deliver across different tones, formats, and ideas. Your portfolio is proof that you're not a one-laugh wonder. It's your comedic identity on paper.

The good news? You don't have to build it alone. With ChatGPT, you can accelerate the creative process, test new formats, refine your jokes, and fill in the gaps. AI doesn't replace your talent—it supports it, scaffolds it, and speeds up the journey from blank page to killer sample.

Here's how to build a well-rounded, eye-catching comedy portfolio using AI as your virtual writers' room.

1. Choose the Right Mix of Materials

A strong comedy portfolio often includes:

- **One original pilot** (your voice, your concept, your characters)
- **One spec episode** (your take on an existing show)
- **A character-driven short (5–10 pages)** or sketch
- **Optional:** digital shorts, comedic monologues, essays, or stand-up-style material

Your portfolio should show both consistency (your voice) and flexibility (your range).

Ask ChatGPT:

"What combination of writing samples would show off my skills as a sitcom writer and also my sketch comedy background?"

2. Write Multiple Original Pilots in Different Comedy Subgenres

Don't just write one type of funny. Show that you can write:

- A grounded workplace comedy
- A family or relationship-based sitcom
- A high-concept or genre-bending show (sci-fi, fantasy, dark comedy)

Try prompts like:

"Give me five original sitcom concepts: one grounded, one absurd, one workplace, one animated, and one romantic comedy."

Then go further:

"Outline a 10-episode arc for this premise."

"Write the cold open for the pilot using character-based humor and a quick visual gag."

"Punch up this pilot scene to match the tone of a show like *The Bear* meets *Brooklyn Nine-Nine*."

3. Generate Spec Episodes That Show You Get TV

Spec episodes (scripts written for existing shows) show that you can write in someone else's voice—an essential skill in any writers' room.

Use ChatGPT to help:

"Give me a plotline for a spec episode of *What We Do in the Shadows* that hasn't been done yet."

"Write an outline for a *Hacks* spec where Deborah has to roast a celebrity she secretly loves."

Then:

"Write a scene from this spec episode with dialogue that captures the tone and rhythm of the show."

4. Build a Sketch Packet or Short Form Comedy Set

Sketch packets are often required for late-night, digital, and variety jobs. A packet might include:

- Topical sketch ideas
- Character monologues
- Parody commercials
- Absurdist or short-form bits

Let ChatGPT help build:

"Give me ten sketch premises that feel like *SNL* or *Key & Peele*."

"Write a 2-minute sketch where a bank robber apologizes too much during the heist."

You can also generate digital shorts or social media-style scripts.

5. Create a Punch-Up Sample or Rewrite Challenge

If you want to be hired as a joke writer or punch-up consultant, include a sample that shows your ability to improve existing material.

Try:

"Here's a scene. Rewrite it with sharper jokes, better pacing, and one running gag."

"Turn this dry dialogue into something worthy of *Arrested Development* or *Veep*."

Include both the original and your punch-up version to show your thought process and results.

6. Include a One-Page Comedic Bio or Personal Statement

Many writers are asked for a "funny bio" or personal statement for fellowships, applications, and submissions.

ChatGPT can help:

"Write a one-page comedic bio about a writer who used to teach improv to lawyers and now writes about emotionally repressed people doing ridiculous things."

Make sure it matches the tone of your portfolio—quirky but professional.

7. Organize and Polish Your Portfolio for Submission

You don't want to just send a folder full of files. Structure matters.

Use this order:

1. Original pilot (best first)
2. Second pilot or spec
3. Sketches or shorts
4. Bio or statement
5. Optional: additional scripts, pitch documents, or outlines

Ask ChatGPT:

"Help me write a short paragraph to introduce this portfolio and explain what connects these samples."

You can also build a digital version using Notion, Google Drive, or a personal website. Make it easy to read, download, and admire.

Building a comedy portfolio doesn't mean waiting months between ideas. With ChatGPT, you can generate new material, test multiple tones, refine existing work, and grow your writing body fast. It gives you the space to try, fail, learn, and laugh—all while filling your folder with real, readable proof that you're a working comedy writer, not just an aspiring one.

So don't wait for permission. Start building. Start compiling. Start sharing. Your voice is funny. Your samples just need to *prove it.*

You Wrote a Comedy Series Today—Now Write the Next One Tomorrow

Take a moment. You wrote an entire comedy series—from idea to finished draft, from concept to character arcs, punchlines to pilot script. Maybe it took one day. Maybe a week. Maybe longer. Doesn't matter. You built something that didn't exist before, something that made you laugh and might one day make others laugh too. And now? Now you do it again.

That's the real secret behind being a working comedy writer. Not writing *once*. Writing *again*. Building a second world. Finding new voices. New dynamics. New formats. The truth is, your first series proves you can do it. Your second proves you're a writer.

This chapter is about momentum. About taking everything you just learned, using the tools that helped you finish, and carrying it straight into your next idea—without overthinking, without hesitation, and without waiting for someone to tell you it's time.

Because it is.

1. Creativity Is a Muscle—And You Just Warmed It Up

Finishing one comedy series has already done most of the heavy lifting. You know how to:

- Build a beat sheet.
- Create a logline and concept.
- Outline an arc for a season.
- Create strong character dynamics.
- Finish a script.
- Use AI to assist, expand, and polish.

That's not theoretical knowledge anymore. That's lived-in skill. And the best way to keep it sharp? *Use it again, immediately.*

Try this:

"Give me 5 original comedy series concepts in completely different genres: workplace, sci-fi, historical, animated, and musical."

Pick one. Just start. The barrier is gone.

2. Keep What Worked, Improve What Didn't

Every creative process has friction. Maybe you got stuck on the midpoint. Maybe character voices blended. Maybe your cold open took 3 hours to land.

Good. That's gold. Use that awareness to make your next series smoother:

- If structure was hard, build the beat sheet *first*.
- If tone was fuzzy, write a sample scene *before* committing.

- If the dialogue dragged, spend time designing voice and rhythm early on.

Ask ChatGPT:

"What were the strengths of my last comedy script? What elements could I make stronger in my next one?"

You're not starting from zero. You're building from insight.

3. Try a New Format or Flavor

Maybe your last project was a grounded single-cam. Go surreal. Go animated. Write a web series. Try a sketch show format. Write the sitcom you swore you'd never write.

Creative speed doesn't mean repeating yourself—it means experimenting *fast*.

Prompt:

"Give me a concept for a short-form comedy series told entirely through video calls."

Or:

"I just wrote a family comedy. What's a total tonal opposite I can write next?"

Break the mold you just built.

4. Build a Practice of Starting

You don't have to finish every series you start. But you should *start* often. Each one sharpens your instinct, hones your pacing, and deepens your voice.

Use ChatGPT like a story gym:

"Let's build a new series from scratch. Start with a logline about an accidental cult leader."

"Now give me the main cast, tone guide, and a Season 1 episode list."

Do that every day for a week. You'll end up with seven raw concepts—one might be your next favorite.

5. Stack the Work—Don't Stall It

You've built a system now:

1. Idea
2. Logline
3. Beat Sheet
4. Cold Open
5. Draft
6. Punch-up
7. Polish
8. Package

That's your personal production pipeline. Don't wait to finish one to start the next. While one is being edited, outline another. While one is being pitched, draft a third.

Ask ChatGPT:

"Help me map out a 3-month plan to write and polish three original comedy series samples for my portfolio."

Keep your pipeline moving. Keep the ideas hot.

6. You're Not Starting Over—You're Levelling Up

Every new show you write builds on the last:

- Your characters get richer.
- Your dialogue gets snappier.
- Your world-building gets faster.
- Your structure becomes instinctual.
- Your rewrites go deeper.
- Your confidence goes up.

And eventually, the thing that once felt impossible—writing an entire comedy series—becomes *just what you do now.*

Final Thought

You wrote a comedy series today. That's not a small thing. That's creative follow-through. That's craft. That's a win.

But the real magic? It's in the next one. And the one after that. Because the only way to become a prolific, working comedy writer is to *act like one now.*

So open a new page. Type a new title. And when the idea hits—however weird, small, wild, or brilliant—don't overthink it.

Just write the next one.

I hope you found inspiration within these pages. If you liked this book, please leave a review where you bought it. Thank you from the author.

About the Author

Andrew Parry is a writer and filmmaker with a profound love for film, particularly the genre of science fiction. His passion for the limitless possibilities of sci-fi drives both his storytelling and his creative vision. For Andrew, science fiction is more than just a genre—it's a way to explore the boundaries of human imagination, the future of technology, and the mysteries of the universe. Through his writing and filmmaking, Andrew seeks to create narratives that transport audiences to worlds filled with awe, wonder, and the thrill of discovery.

Read more at https://lonetrail.blog.

www.ingramcontent.com/pod-product-compliance
Lightning Source LLC
LaVergne TN
LVHW082341200926
848481LV00012B/3414